REDISCOVERED
LEWIS CARROLL
PUZZLES

REDISCOVERED LEWIS CARROLL PUZZLES

Newly Compiled and
Edited by

Edward Wakeling

DOVER PUBLICATIONS, INC.
NEW YORK

Copyright

Copyright © 1995 by Edward Wakeling.
Extracts from Lewis Carroll's previously unpublished letters and papers copyright © 1995 by the Trustees of the C. L. Dodgson Estate.

Published in Canada by General Publishing Company, Ltd., 30 Lesmill Road, Don Mills, Toronto, Ontario.
Published in the United Kingdom by Constable and Company, Ltd., 3 The Lanchesters, 162–164 Fulham Palace Road, London W6 9ER.

Bibliographical Note

Rediscovered Lewis Carroll Puzzles is a new work, first published by Dover Publications, Inc., in 1995.

Library of Congress Cataloging-in-Publication Data

Carroll, Lewis, 1832–1898.
   Rediscovered Lewis Carroll puzzles ; newly compiled and edited by Edward Wakeling.
       p.   cm.
   Includes bibliographical references (p.   –   ).
   ISBN 0-486-28861-7 (pbk.)
   1. Mathematical recreations.   I. Wakeling, Edward.   II. Title.
QA95.C334   1995
793.73—dc20   95-30151
                                                                                  CIP

Manufactured in the United States of America
Dover Publications, Inc., 31 East 2nd Street, Mineola, N.Y. 11501

Acknowledgements

I am extremely grateful to Philip Dodgson Jaques, Senior Trustee of the C. L. Dodgson Estate, for his kind permission to use extracts from previously unpublished letters, papers and diary entries.

I have used further material from the Bartholomew Price archive, and for this I again offer my sincere thanks to Dr. Francis V. Price.

In the first book of *Lewis Carroll's Games and Puzzles,* I was ably assisted by Alan Weissman at Dover Publications, and I take this opportunity to express my thanks to him for his help and support.

Once again, I offer my sincere thanks to Mark Richards for reading through the contents of this book, checking the solutions and offering valuable advice.

Publisher's Note:
To American Readers

In several puzzles, reference is made to British money. In the new system of currency, introduced in 1971, a hundred pence (plural of "penny" and abbreviated "p.") make a pound (indicated by the symbol "£" placed before the number, as with American dollars). In the older system, pence had a different value and were indicated by the symbol "d." There was also a major intermediate denomination called a "shilling" ("s."), as well as several other denominations made of combinations of the foregoing. This system is more fully explained in puzzle 31.

American readers should also note that dates in Great Britain are generally written in the order "day-month-year."

Contents

The Solutions to the Puzzles   63

Introduction

Here is the second volume of games and puzzles selected almost exclusively from the writings and inventions of Lewis Carroll. Some puzzles may have come from other sources, but we know that all of them were used by Lewis Carroll to entertain his young friends and colleagues. He was a pioneer in the realm of recreational mathematics, and intended to publish his own book of games and puzzles. Unfortunately, his preoccupation with many other writing projects prevented this from happening. Throughout his life he collected a mass of puzzles, a great many of which were of his own invention. A few were published in his lifetime, but the vast majority remained on slips of paper or survived only in letters to his friends. This is a further compilation of these delightful and varied puzzles, some being published here for the first time.

Since the first volume (*Lewis Carroll's Games and Puzzles*) appeared, I have been asked to suggest an age range for which these games and puzzles are most appropriate and to whom they are most likely to appeal. I reply in a manner characteristic of Lewis Carroll: in my opinion, they will be enjoyed by children of ages five to ninety-five, and also by some adults. I have tried them out with just such an age range, and find that they are eagerly and successfully tackled. Clearly, some of the problems require a mathematical competence beyond that of most five-year-olds. My advice is to be selective; choose games and puzzles that appeal to you. If they prove to be too difficult, never mind; there are plenty more to choose from. I would not want to underestimate the competence of young people. In my experience, many have a highly developed intuitive sense for solving these problems and welcome the challenge.

As before, I have included my solutions. I should add that Lewis Carroll did not always leave us with his solutions, so there is a strong possibility that you may be able to improve upon my attempts.

There is one overriding principle that should be adhered to at all times. In attempting these games and puzzles, it is imperative that you experience enjoyment and fun. I hope you do.

EDWARD WAKELING

THE GAMES AND PUZZLES

1

Why Is a Raven Like a Writing-Desk?

"Your hair wants cutting," said the Hatter. He had been looking at Alice for some time with great curiosity, and this was his first speech.

"You should learn not to make personal remarks," Alice said with some severity: "it's very rude."

The Hatter opened his eyes very wide on hearing this; but all he *said* was "Why is a raven like a writing-desk?"

"Come, we shall have some fun now!" thought Alice. "I'm glad they've begun asking riddles—I believe I can guess that," she added aloud.

"Do you mean that you think you can find out the answer to it?" said the March Hare.

"Exactly so," said Alice.

And so the Mad Tea-Party in Lewis Carroll's *Alice's Adventures in Wonderland* continues. For some time the conversation turns to the Hatter's watch, which has been liberally smeared with butter by the March Hare, and the Dormouse sleeps. Then, for no apparent reason, the Hatter's riddle resurfaces:

"Have you guessed the riddle yet?" the Hatter said, turning to Alice again.

"No, I give it up," Alice replied. "What's the answer?"

"I haven't the slightest idea," said the Hatter.

"Nor I," said the March Hare.

This riddle with "no answer" has been the subject of many puzzles and competitions to find the best possible solution.

Why do you think a raven is like a writing-desk?

You will find some possible solutions to this riddle at the end of this book, together with the answers to the other problems and puzzles that appear on the following pages.

A Rebus Letter

Apart from being the writer of many books, Lewis Carroll was an avid writer of letters. He kept a letter register, and his last-known entry is numbered 98,721. The register recorded both incoming and outgoing letters; nevertheless, it has been estimated that he wrote nearly 50,000 letters in his lifetime, many of them to children and written in the same delightful tone as the *Alice* books.

The daughter of the postmaster of Merton College, Oxford University, was named Georgina "Ina" Watson, and sometime in 1869 Lewis Carroll sent her a rebus letter (a letter with some of the words replaced by pictures). The letter is signed "CLD," which are the initials of Lewis Carroll's real name, Charles Lutwidge Dodgson. It is reproduced here; can you discover the contents of this letter?

However somehow 👁 got into the 🏠, 🤚 there a 🐈 met me, 🖐 took me for a ⬛ a 🐱, and pelted me with ✂️🖌, 🥖🥐🏺, 🤚🥒 . Of course 👁 ran into the street again, 🤚 a 🐕 met me 🖐 took me for a 🛒, 🖐 dragged me all the way 2 the 🏚, 🗑 the worst of all was when a 🛒 met me 🖐 took me for a 🐎 . I was harnessed 2 it, 🖐 had 2 draw it miles and miles, all the way 2 Merrow. So U C I couldn't get 2 the room where U were.

However I was glad to hear U were hard at work

learning the

	2	3	4	5
2	4	6	8	10
3	6	9	12	15
4	8	12	16	20
5	10	15	20	25

for a birthday treat.

I had just time 2 look into the kitchen, and your birthday feast getting ready, a nice of crusts, bones, pills, cotton-bobbins, and rhabarb and magnesia— "Now," I thought, "she will be happy!" and with a I went on my way—
Your aff.te friend
CLD

A Spiral Letter

In August 1878, Lewis Carroll visited the Hull family, who were staying at Eastbourne. He became great friends with the daughters, Alice, Agnes, Eveline and Jessie, taking them on outings, walks and rowing trips. A few weeks later he had the idea of producing a small, privately printed booklet containing personal riddles and puzzles for the Hull sisters. He titled the book *Remarks on the Victims,* and by the following summer he had produced a manuscript version, which he gave to Agnes on 23 August 1879. He noted in his diary: "Agnes carried off the little MS book . . . and probably dropped it in the road: at all events it is lost."

This spiral letter, addressed to Agnes and written on 22 October 1878, may have been included in the lost volume. The book itself gets a mention; clearly, Agnes was getting impatient about receiving it. On 16 November, Lewis Carroll sent Agnes another letter reminding her that patience is a virtue. He also adds that he has thought of a new conundrum for the book: "Why is Agnes like a thermometer?" "Because she won't rise when it's cold."

Can you discover the contents of this letter?

The Captive Queen

A captive Queen and her son and daughter were shut up in the top room of a very high tower. Outside their window was a pulley with a rope round it, and a basket fastened at each end of the rope of equal weight. They managed to escape with the help of this and a weight they found in the room, quite safely. It would have been dangerous for any of them to come down if they weighed more than 15 lbs. more than the contents of the lower basket, for they would do so too quick, and they also managed not to weigh less either.

The one basket coming down would naturally of course draw the other up.

How did they do it?

The Queen weighed 195 lbs., daughter 165, son 90, and the weight 75.

This may not be an original puzzle invented by Lewis Carroll, but we know that he used it to entertain his guests on a number of occasions. His biographer and nephew, Stuart Dodgson Collingwood, included it in a compilation of other works by his uncle in a book titled *The Lewis Carroll Picture Book* (T. Fisher Unwin, 1899).

This particular problem comes with an additional question:

The Queen had with her in the room, besides her son and daughter and the weight, a pig weighing 60 lbs., a dog 45 lbs., and a cat 30. These have to be brought down safely, too, with the same restriction. The weight can come down any way, of course.

. . . there must be someone at each end to put the animals into and out of the baskets.

What are the solutions to these two problems?

5

A New Way to Pay Old Debts

This extract comes from *Sylvie and Bruno,* Lewis Carroll's last children's story:

"Come in!" [called the Professor]

"Only the tailor, Sir, with your little bill," said a meek voice outside the door.

"Ah, well, I can soon settle *his* business," the Professor said to the children, "if you'll just wait a minute. How much is it, this year, my man?" The tailor had come in while he was speaking.

"Well, it's been doubling so many years, you see," the tailor replied, a little gruffly, "and I think I'd like the money now. It's two thousand pounds, it is!"

"Oh, that's nothing!" the Professor carelessly remarked, feeling in his pocket, as if he always carried at least *that* amount about with him. "But wouldn't you like to wait just another year, and make it *four* thousand? Just think how rich you'd be! Why, you might be a *King,* if you liked!"

"I don't know as I'd care about being a *King,*" the man said thoughtfully. "But it *dew* sound a powerful sight o' money! Well, I think I'll wait——"

"Of course, you will," said the Professor. "There's good sense in *you,* I see. Good-day to you, my man!"

"Will you ever have to pay him that four thousand pounds?" Sylvie asked as the door closed on the departing creditor.

"*Never,* my child!" the Professor replied emphatically. "He'll go on doubling it, till he dies. You see, it's *always* worth while waiting another year, to get twice as much money!"

If the original bill was for £31.25, how long had the tailor been doubling the Professor's account?

If the bill is doubled for the next:

  (a) ten years;
  (b) twenty years;
  (c) thirty years;

how much will the Professor owe on each occasion?

A similar problem is worthy of investigation. If you put 1p. on a corner square of a chessboard, and then put 2p. on the next square, and 4p. on the next square, and keep doubling the amount on each successive square until the chessboard is completely covered, how much will there be on the 64th square?

6

The Day of the Week for Any Given Date

In the issue of *Nature* dated 31 March 1887, Lewis Carroll contributed the following article:

Having hit upon the following method of mentally computing the day of the week for any given date, I send it you in the hope that it may interest some of your readers. I am not a rapid computer myself, and as I find my average time for doing any such question is about 20 seconds, I have little doubt that a rapid computer would not need 15.

Take the given date in 4 portions, viz. the number of centuries, the number of years over, the month, the day of the month.

Compute the following 4 items, adding each, whenever found, to the total of the previous items. When an item or total exceeds 7, divide by 7, and keep the remainder only.

The Century-Item: For Old Style (which ended September 2, 1752) subtract from 18. The New Style (which began September 14) divide by 4, take overplus from 3, multiply remainder by 2. [Editor's note: the century-item is the first two digits of the year; e.g., for 1832, take 18.]

The Year-Item: Add together the number of dozens, the overplus, and the number of 4's in the overplus.

The Month-Item: If it begins or ends with a vowel, subtract the number, denoting its place in the year, from 10. This, plus its number of days, gives the item for the following month. The item for January is "0"; for February or March (the third month), "3"; for December (the 12th month), "12." [Editor's note: in other words, the required numbers, after division by seven, are as follows: January, 0; February, 3; March, 3; April, 6; May, 1; June, 4; July, 6; August, 2; September, 5; October, 0; November, 3; December, 5.]

The Day-Item: is the day of the month.

The total, thus reached, must be corrected, by deducting "1" (first adding 7, if the total be "0"), if the date be January or February in a Leap Year: remembering that every year, divisible by 4, is a Leap Year, excepting only the century-years, in New Style, when the number of centuries is *not* so divisible (e.g. 1800).

The final result gives the day of the week, "0" meaning Sunday, "1" meaning Monday, and so on.

EXAMPLES

1783, September 18

17, divided by 4, leaves "1" over; 1 from 3 gives "2"; twice 2 is "4."

83 is 6 dozen and 11, giving 17; plus 2 gives 19, i.e. (dividing by 7) "5." Total 9, i.e. "2."

The item for August is "8 from 10," i.e. "2"; so, for September, it is "2 plus 3," i.e. "5." Total 7, i.e. "0," which goes out.

18 gives "4." Answer, *"Thursday."*

1676, February 23

16 from 18 gives "2."

76 is 6 dozen and 4, giving 10; plus 1 gives 11, i.e. "4." Total "6."

The item for February is "3." Total 9, i.e. "2."

23 gives "2." Total "4."

Correction for Leap Year gives "3." Answer, *"Wednesday."*

Here are some dates for you to determine the day of the week:

(a) 27 January 1832 (Lewis Carroll's birthday)
(b) 22 December 1861 (the day Lewis Carroll was ordained Deacon)
(c) 4 July 1862 (the day of the boat-trip during which the tale of *Alice's Adventures* was first told)
(d) 14 January 1898 (Lewis Carroll's death at Guildford)
(e) 20 June 1750 (death of Lewis Carroll's great-great-grandfather, Rev. Christopher Dodgson)
(f) 4 May 1852 (Alice Liddell's birthday)

Try some of your own dates.

7

A Geometrical Paradox

Among Lewis Carroll's papers at the time of his death was an investigation of a famous geometrical paradox in which a shape made from four pieces appears to gain in area when the pieces are assembled in a certain way. These papers are now in the Parrish Collection at Princeton University, U.S.A.

The four pieces A, B, C and D, which make up the square of area 8 × 8 = 64 square units, is transformed into a rectangle of apparent area 5 × 13 = 65 square units. Where does the extra square unit come from?

The original paradox appears to have been published in 1868 by Schlomilch.

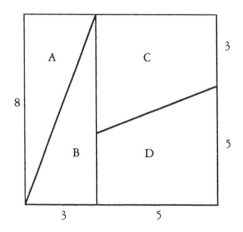

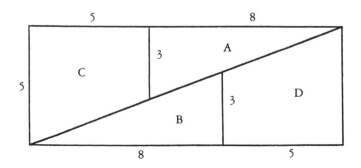

8

The Rule of Three

Lewis Carroll, or to use his real name, the Reverend Charles Lutwidge Dodgson, was the mathematical lecturer at Christ Church, Oxford University, from 1855 to 1881. He gave tutorials to the undergraduates and often checked their mathematical and logical competence by trying out puzzles and problems that he had devised for them. One of his favourite problems concerned "the rule of three," better known as proportion and inverse proportion. Such elementary problems featured in his own mathematical studies while he was at Rugby School before he became an undergraduate in 1851. The mathematical textbook he used during his school days still survives containing a personal inscription in Latin, which roughly translates as "This book belongs to Charles Lutwidge Dodgson; hands off!" The book he used was Francis Walkingame's *The Tutor's Assistant; Being a Compendium of Arithmetic,* published in London in the eighteenth century but reprinted many times. The rule of three is described in this book as follows:

RULE OF THREE INVERSE

Inverse proportion is, when more requires less, and less requires more. More requires less, is when the third term is greater than the first, and requires the fourth term to be less than the second. And less requires more, is when the third term is less than the first, and requires the fourth term to be greater than the second.

13

RULE: Multiply the first and second terms together and divide the product by the third; the quotient will bear such proportion to the second as the first does to the third.

Don't panic! I think that Lewis Carroll appreciated that, in an attempt to clarify a mathematical rule, the result is often very difficult to comprehend at first reading. He echoes this experience in *Alice's Adventures in Wonderland*. The Duchess is talking to Alice in the Queen's Croquet-Ground:

"Only mustard isn't a bird," Alice remarked.

"Right, as usual," said the Duchess: "what a clear way you have of putting things!"

"It's a mineral, I *think*," said Alice.

"Of course it is," said the Duchess, who seemed ready to agree to everything that Alice said: "there's a large mustard-mine near here. And the moral of that is—'The more there is of mine, the less there is of yours.' "

"Oh, I know!" exclaimed Alice, who had not attended to this last remark. "It's a vegetable. It doesn't look like one, but it is."

"I quite agree with you," said the Duchess, "and the moral of that is—'Be what you would seem to be'—or, if you'd like it put more simply—'Never imagine yourself not to be otherwise than what it might appear to others that what you were or might have been was not otherwise than what you had been would have appeared to them to be otherwise.' "

Walkingame's textbook gives some written examples to put the rule of three more clearly:

If 8 men can do a piece of work in 12 days; in how many days can 16 men perform the same?

Solution:

It is evident by the nature of the question that the answer is days, we therefore put 12 days for the third term, as the answer will be less than the third term, because 16 men will do more work than 8 men, therefore we put the least in the second place, and the remaining term in the first place.

As 16 men : 8 men :: 12 days : *6 days*

[Calculated as follows: $8 \times 12 / 16 = 6$ days]

Lewis Carroll's problem, which he frequently gave to his under-graduates, was:

If it takes 4 men, 1 day to build a wall, how long does it take 60,000 men to build a similar wall?

A variation which he also used was:

If a cat can kill a rat in a minute, how long would it be killing 60,000 rats?

The answers are not quite as mathematical al as they seem, but based upon reasonable logic.

14

9

The Monkey and Weight Problem

In 1893, Lewis Carroll circulated a problem among his colleagues at Oxford University and was surprised to find that they had differing views about the solution. The problem is one that would be difficult to test practically; it has to be resolved using the known rules of motion, and it concerns a monkey and a weight. This is how Lewis Carroll stated the problem:

A rope is supposed to be hung over a wheel fixed to the roof of a building; at one end of the rope a weight is fixed, which exactly counterbalances a monkey which is hanging on the other end. Suppose that the monkey begins to climb the rope, what will be the result?

He went on to suggest that the rope was perfectly flexible and the pulley frictionless.

Lewis Carroll was amused to find eminent mathematicians and scientists conflicting in their responses. On 21 December 1893, he wrote in his diary:

> Got Prof. Clifton's answer to the "Monkey and Weight" problem. It is very curious, the different views taken by good mathematicians. Price says the weight goes *up*, with increasing velocity. Clifton (and Harcourt) that it goes *up*, at the same rate as the monkey, while Sampson says that it goes *down!*

Professor Robert Bellamy Clifton was a renowned scientist who held the Chair of Experimental Philosophy at Oxford University. Professor Bartholomew "Bat" Price was Lewis Carroll's mathematical tutor, Fellow and later Master of Pembroke College. Augustus Vernon Harcourt was Lee's Reader in Chemistry at Christ Church and a lifelong friend of Lewis Carroll. The Reverend Edward Francis Sampson was Lewis Carroll's assistant mathematical tutor at Christ Church and also a long-standing friend.

What do you think happens to the weight as the monkey climbs up the rope?

10

Crossing the River

Four gentleman and their wives wanted to cross the river in a boat that would not hold more than two at a time.

The conditions were, that no gentleman must leave his wife on the bank unless with only women or by herself, and also that some one must always bring the boat back.

How did they do it?

This is probably not an original problem invented by Lewis Carroll, but it is clear that he liked logical puzzles of this kind and often used them to entertain his friends. Another favourite was the famous river-crossing problem involving the fox, the goose and the bag of corn (see problem 26 in *Lewis Carroll's Games and Puzzles*) which he often gave to child-friends to solve. The problem of the gentlemen and their wives was given to his colleagues at Oxford.

Castle Croquet

"Can you play croquet?"

The soldiers were silent, and looked at Alice, as the question was evidently meant for her.

"Yes!" shouted Alice.

"Come on, then!" roared the Queen.

Lewis Carroll invented a variation on the normal game of Croquet played on grass in which the arches become castles and the balls become either soldiers or sentinels. The rules were printed in 1863 following a series of trial games played with the three eldest daughters of Dean Liddell, Lorina, Alice and Edith. Originally intended for five players, he modified the game for four players and published new rules in 1866. This version was also published in *Aunt Judy's Magazine* the following year, and it is this version which is reproduced here.

Castle Croquet
for four players

```
            .
            :
           . .
            3
. . . :  2     4  :  . . .
            1
           . .
            :
            .
```

Key: . peg; : door; . . gate

RULES

I.

This game requires 8 balls, 8 arches, and 4 pegs. 4 of the balls are called "soldiers;" the others "sentinels." The arches and pegs are set up as in the figure, making 4 "castles," and each player has a castle, a soldier, and a sentinel. Before the game begins, each player places his sentinel within a mallet's length of his peg, and does the same with his soldier when his turn comes to play.

(N.B. The distance from one gate to the next should be 6 or 8 yards, and the distance from the gate to the door, or from the door to the peg, 2 or 3 yards.)

If a sentinel goes through the gate of his castle, in the direction *from* his peg, he is said to "leave" the castle; when next he goes through it in the opposite direction, he is said to "re-enter" it, and so on. A sentinel, that has not left his castle, is said to be "on duty;" if he leaves it, he is said to be "off duty;" if he re-enters it, to be "on duty" again, and so on.

To begin the game, the owner of Castle No. 1 places and plays his soldier, and then plays his sentinel; then the owner of Castle No. 2, and so on. Each player has to bring his soldier out of his castle (by playing it through the gate), and with it "invade" the other castles in order (e.g., No. 3 has to invade castles 4, 1, 2), re-enter his own castle, and lastly, touch his peg, his sentinel being "on duty" at the time; and whoever does all this first wins. To "invade" a castle, the soldier must enter at the gate, go through the door (either way), touch the peg, and go out at the gate again.

If an invading soldier touch, or be touched by, the sentinel "on duty" of the castle he is invading, he becomes "prisoner," and is placed behind the peg. He may be released by the sentinel going "off duty," or by his own sentinel "on duty" coming and touching the peg: in the latter case, his sentinel is at once replaced as at the beginning of the game. The released soldier is "in hand" till his next turn, when he is placed as at the beginning of the game.

When a soldier goes through an arch, or touches a peg, "in order," or when a sentinel takes a prisoner, he may be played again. Also when a sentinel leaves, or re-enters, his castle, he may be played again, but may not exercise either of these privileges twice in one turn.

If the ball played touch another (neither of them being a sentinel "on duty"), the player may "take two" off the ball so touched, but must not move it in doing so. If, however, the ball so touched be his own sentinel "off duty," he may take a croquet of any kind, as in the ordinary game. He may not "take two," or take a croquet twice in one turn off the same ball, unless he has meanwhile gone through an arch, or touched a peg "in order."

N.B. The following arrangement of the 8 balls as soldiers and sentinels will be found convenient:

CASTLE	SOLDIER	SENTINEL
I.	Blue	Pink
II.	Black	Yellow
III.	Brown	Orange
IV.	Green	Red

ADVICE TO THE PLAYER

As it is not easy, in a new game, to see at once what is the best method of play in the various situations that may occur, the following suggestions may be of use to the player.

There are two distinct methods of play, which you may adopt in this game, and each has its own special advantages: the one consists in keeping your sentinel "on duty;" the other, in bringing it "off duty."

In the first method, your sentinel remains constantly at home, except when your soldier is in danger of being taken prisoner, when it is played up to the peg of the castle you are invading, so as to be ready to release your soldier. In this method, the best position for your sentinel is opposite to the centre of your gate, and a ball's width from it, so that if a soldier, trying to invade your castle, should touch it, it must have previously passed through the gate. From this position it is easy to take a prisoner in any part of your castle by the following rule: Play your sentinel just through the gate; this gives you another turn, in which you play it in again, getting as near as possible to the invading soldier; this gives you another turn, in which you may take it prisoner. The same process may be employed for playing your sentinel up to the peg of the castle you are invading, if it should happen that you cannot play it straight for the peg. This process, however, must not be employed when you have a prisoner in your castle, as it would be released by your sentinel going out.

In the second method, your sentinel keeps with your soldier: when playing your soldier, you carry the sentinel along with it, through one or more arches, by raking "loose croquets" or "split strokes;" and when your soldier can do no more, you either play your sentinel close up to it, ready for the next turn, or, if your soldier is in danger of being taken prisoner, you "take two" off it, getting as close as possible to the enemy's sentinel in the first stroke, and driving it to a safe distance in the second.

The first method is the safest, when any one of the other players is better than yourself, as it enables you to prevent his entering your castle and so to delay him; but as soon as all the players, whom you have reason to fear, have passed through your castle, you had better bring your sentinel "off duty," and help your soldier.

The second method enables you to make rapid progress in invading the other castles: you can also take prisoners almost as easily as in the first method, by "taking two" off your soldier, getting near your gate in the first stroke, and entering your castle in the second: this gives you another turn, in which you may take a prisoner. It has, however, the disadvantage of loss of time if your soldier should be made a prisoner, as in this case your sentinel has to go home, get "on duty," and return, before it can release your soldier.

If your soldier is taken prisoner, and you release it by touching the enemy's peg with your sentinel, you are in a position in which you may often retard the other players: first, by placing your sentinel (which is done directly after the release) in a line between your peg and an invading soldier which is aiming at it; secondly, by placing your soldier (which is done when your next turn comes) close to your sentinel, playing it so as to drive your sentinel in the direction of an invading soldier, and then taking it prisoner.

It evidently follows from this that, when you have yourself taken a prisoner, and happen to be invading the castle from which it came, you should not wait till the enemy's sentinel has touched your peg and so released the prisoner, but you should yourself release it (as soon as the enemy's sentinel has nearly reached your peg) by playing your own sentinel out through your gate and in again: in this case the sentinel, which was on its way to your peg, cannot be carried back at once, but must be played all the way home.

In "taking two" off a ball you may, if you choose, play your own ball so as only just to move it, and then strike it in the direction of the other, and thus drive it to a distance. This has nearly the same effect as the "loose croquet" of the ordinary game, but with this difference, that it does not give you the right of playing again.

If a soldier, about to invade your castle, is lying near your gate, you may take it prisoner thus: Play your sentinel out, near the soldier; then hit it with your sentinel, and "take two" off it, so as only just to move your ball, taking care to have the soldier in a line between your sentinel and your gate; then drive both in together; this gives you another turn, in which you may take it prisoner.

More Doublets

Lewis Carroll's Games and Puzzles included Lewis Carroll's own word-game "Doublets," with a number of examples. He produced many more examples, however, and I am taking the opportunity to include some more here. By way of a reminder, here is a worked example. The rules are that you may change only one letter at a time, the remaining letters keeping their position, and all the link-words in the chain must be real words that are found in a standard dictionary.

Make BREAD from FLOUR

> FLOUR
> f l o o r
> f l o o d
> b l o o d
> b r o o d
> b r o a d
> BREAD

If you would like a few very easy ones to start you off, then try these:

BAT into MAN; TEA into POT; CAR into VAN; MUM into DAD

Here is a selection from Lewis Carroll's third and fourth "Doublets" competitions, which were published in *Vanity Fair* between November 1879 and April 1880:

> Send JOE to ANN
> Change TILES for SLATE
> Pluck ACORN from STALK
> HOAX a FOOL
> Bring JACK to JILL
> Serve COFFEE after DINNER
> Row BOAT with OARS
> Change NOUN to VERB
> Bring SHIP into DOCK
> PLANT BEANS
> Raise UNIT to FOUR
> Prove LIES to be TRUE
> Turn HORSE out to GRASS
> OPEN GATE
> CRY OUT
> Send BOWLER to WICKET

13

Names in Poems

At Christmas 1861, Lewis Carroll gave the three daughters of Dean Liddell a copy of Catherine Sinclair's *Holiday House,* and included within it a short poem which identifies not only the title of the book, but also the names of the three sisters. What were their names?

> Little maidens, when you look
> On this little story-book,
> Reading with attentive eye
> Its enticing history,
> Never think that hours of play
> Are your only HOLIDAY,
> And that in a HOUSE of joy
> Lessons serve but to annoy:
> If in any HOUSE you find
> Children of a gentle mind,
> Each the others pleasing ever—
> Each the others vexing never—
> Daily work and pastime daily
> In their order taking gaily—
> Then be very sure that they
> Have a life of HOLIDAY.

In 1885, Lewis Carroll published a series of puzzles, which had appeared in *The Monthly Packet* as individual "knots," in a book called *A Tangled Tale.* Some of these puzzles are reproduced later in this volume (see numbers 39–41). The book contains a poem dedicated to one of his child-friends; can you discover her name, which is hidden within the verses?

> Beloved Pupil! Tamed by thee,
>   Addish=, Subtrac=, Multiplica=tion,
> Division, Fractions, Rule of Three,
>   Attest thy deft manipulation!
>
> Then onward! Let the voice of Fame
>   From Age to Age repeat thy story,
> Till thou hast won thyself a name
>   Exceeding even Euclid's glory.

Lewis Carroll was fond of giving copies of his books to friends, and often composed some verses for the recipient, which he inscribed in the book. On many occasions these poems were acrostics; they hid the name of the person to whom the book was given. In some of his books, he printed a set of dedicatory acrostic verses, as in the previous example.

The following poem was inscribed by hand in a copy of *Rhyme? and Reason?* which he presented to the Misses Drury. What were their names?

"Maidens! If you love the tale,
  If you love the Snark,
Need I urge you, spread the sail,
Now, while freshly blows the gale,
  In your ocean-barque!

"English Maidens love renown,
  Enterprise, and fuss!"
Laughingly those Maidens frown;
Laughingly, with eyes cast down;
  And they answer thus:

"English Maidens fear to roam.
  Much we dread the dark;
Much we dread what ills might come,
If we left our English home,
  Even for a Snark!"

Lewis Carroll's book of humorous verses, *Rhyme? and Reason?*, contained his epic nonsense poem, "The Hunting of the Snark," referred to in the acrostic above.

Anagrams

In the Mad Tea-Party scene from *Alice's Adventures in Wonderland*, the Dormouse tells a story about three sisters at the bottom of a treacle-well. One was named "Lacie." This is an anagram for "Alice"; that is, the letters are just rearranged.

Lewis Carroll enjoyed working out anagrams, from time to time based upon the famous people of the day. In 1868 he sent to a newspaper for publication an anagram for the name of William Ewart Gladstone, who first became British prime minister in that year. Although it was not published at the time, this anagram, and many others, survived on scraps of paper. His anagram for the name of Gladstone is as follows:

Wilt tear down all images?

He also invented two other anagrams for the same name:

A wild man will go at trees.

Wild agitator! Means well.

For the name of Edward Vaughan Kenealy, a notorious Victorian barrister known for his violent conduct in trials, he devised the following:

Ah! We dread an ugly knave.

Here is an anagram, invented by Lewis Carroll, for the name of a famous female personage of the Victorian era. Who was she?

Flit on, cheering angel.

The Flower Riddle

This time [Alice] came upon a large flower-bed, with a border of daisies, and a willow-tree growing in the middle.

"O Tiger-lily!" said Alice, addressing herself to one that was waving gracefully about in the wind, "I *wish* you could talk!"

"We *can* talk," said the Tiger-lily, "when there's anybody worth talking to."

Three particular friends of Lewis Carroll were Harriett, Mary and Georgina Watson, the daughters of the Reverend George William Watson. A number of puzzles and games were invented for this trio, including this poetic riddle:

> Tell me truly, Maidens three,
> Where can all these wonders be?
> Where tooth of lion, eye of ox,
> And foot of cat and tail of fox,
> With ear of mouse and tongue of hound
> And beard of goat, together bound
> With hair of Maiden, strew the ground.

Can you identify these wonders?

16

Feeding the Cat

In the December 1870 issue of *Aunt Judy's Magazine,* edited by Mrs. Gatty, some "Puzzles from Wonderland" appeared, contributed by the editor's friend and acquaintance, Lewis Carroll. The fifth puzzle was a riddle, set within a verse that went as follows:

> Three sisters at breakfast were feeding the cat,
> The first gave it sole—Puss was grateful for that:
> The next gave it salmon—which Puss thought a treat:
> The third gave it herring—which Puss wouldn't eat.
> (Explain the conduct of the cat.)

The Sun and the Moon

Another "Puzzle from Wonderland" that appeared in *Aunt Judy's Magazine* concerned a dialogue between the sun and the moon. Again, the riddle is written in verse:

> Said the Moon to the Sun,
>   "Is the daylight begun?"
> Said the Sun to the Moon,
>   "Not a minute too soon."
>
> "You're a Full Moon," said he.
>   She replied with a frown,
> "Well! I never *did* see
>   So uncivil a clown!"

(Query. Why was the moon so angry?)

18

Tangrams

In a book titled *Amusements in Mathematics,* written by Henry Ernest Dudeney (Thomas Nelson, 1917), the author includes a Chinese puzzle invented by a Mr. Tan and now known as the Tangram. Dudeney writes:

> A few years ago a little book came into my possession, from the library of the late Lewis Carroll, entitled *The Fashionable Chinese Puzzle.* It contains three hundred and twenty-three Tangram designs, mostly nondescript geometrical figures, to be constructed from the seven pieces.

The seven pieces are made from a dissected square, as shown below:

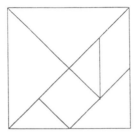

Dudeney goes on to say:

As I have referred to the author of *Alice in Wonderland,* I give also my designs of the March Hare . . . and the Hatter. . . .

Can you assemble the seven Tangram pieces to make these designs?

A Sticky but Polished Riddle

In a letter to Mrs. George MacDonald, written on 3 March 1875, Lewis Carroll added a riddle, which he had just invented, for the entertainment of Mrs. MacDonald's daughters. The riddle was also sent to other child-friends. One recipient, Gaynor Simpson, had difficulty in arriving at a solution, so Carroll sent her two successive answers to the riddle which turned out to be leg-pulls (these are given below). The original riddle hid a two-syllable word connected with the title given above.

> My first lends his aid when I plunge into trade:
> My second in jollifications:
> My whole, laid on thinnish, imparts a neat finish
> To pictorial representations.

The two letters to Gaynor Simpson:

My dear Gaynor,
   So you would like to know the answer to that riddle? Don't be in a hurry to tell it to Amy and Frances: triumph over them for a while!
   My first lends its aid when you plunge into trade.
Gain. Who would go into trade it there were no gain in it?
   My second in jollifications—
Or. (The French for 'gold'—). Your jollifications would be *very* limited if you had no money.
   My whole, laid on thinnish, imparts a neat finish
      To pictorial representations.
Gaynor. Because she will be an ornament to the Shakespeare Charades— only she must be 'laid on thinnish', that is, *there mustn't be too much of her.*

Yours affectionately,
C. L. Dodgson.

My dear Gaynor,
   Forgive me for having sent you a sham answer to begin with.
   My first—*Sea.* It carries the ships of the merchants.
   My second—*Weed.* That is, a cigar, an article much used in jollifications.
   My whole—*Seaweed.* Take a newly painted oil-picture; lay it on its back on the floor, and spread over it, 'thinnish', some wet seaweed. You will find you have 'finished' that picture.

Yours affectionately,
C. L. Dodgson.

20

Anagrammatic Sonnet

In a letter to Maud Standen, written on 18 December 1877, Lewis Carroll included a puzzle which must be the ultimate in "anagrams": a poem of six lines with four anagrams hidden in each line. He did not leave a solution, but various people have attempted to provide all 24 answers, some of which will be found in the solutions section at the end of this book. An extract from the letter to Maud Standen follows:

My dear Miss Standen,

. . . You say croquet has gone quite out of fashion with you; so, perhaps, when this reaches you, it may have come in again. On the chance of which I will enclose a copy of the rules of a game I once invented with the help of my sisters, though perhaps I may have told you about it before. At all events, my "Anagrammatic Sonnet" will be new to you. Each line has four feet, and each foot is an anagram, i.e. the letters of it can be rearranged so as to make one word. Thus there are 24 anagrams, which will occupy your leisure moments for some time, I hope. Remember, I don't limit myself to substantives, as some do. I should consider "we dishwished" a fair anagram.

> As to the war, try elm. I tried.
> The wig cast in, I went to ride.
> "Ring? Yes." We rang. "Let's rap." We don't.
> "O shew her wit!" As yet she won't.
> Saw eel in Rome. Dry one: he's wet.
> I am dry. O forge! Th' rogue! Why a net?

An additional puzzle included in Maud Standen's letter was a compound word to be made from the letters "abcdefgi," which Lewis Carroll described as being as good as the word "summer-house."

The rules for the game of croquet mentioned in this letter are Lewis Carroll's own invention called "Castle Croquet," which can be found in this book, game number 11.

A Charade

Included in the letter to Maud Standen, above, was a riddle in the form of a poetic charade, written for the three youngest Hull sisters, Agnes, Eveline and Jessie. It appears that the youngest of the three had the habit of interposing *"and Jessie"* if any proposal was made that failed to include her, to be certain that she was not left out. Lewis Carroll made use of this characteristic by leaving out the last two words in the poem.

> They both make a roaring—a roaring all night:
> They both are a fisherman-father's delight:
> They are both, when in fury, a terrible sight!
>
> The First nurses tenderly three little hulls,
> To the lullaby-music of shrill-screaming gulls,
> And laughs when they dimple his face with their skulls.
>
> The Second's a tidyish sort of a lad,
> Who behaves pretty well to a man he calls "Dad"
> And earns the remark "Well, he isn't so bad!"
>
> Of the two put together, oh what shall I say?
> 'Tis a time when "to live" means the same as "to play"
> When the busiest person does nothing all day:
>
> When the grave College Don, full of lore inexpressi-
> -ble, puts it all by, and is forced to confess he
> Can think but of Agnes and Evey . . . .

The answer to the riddle is a two-syllable word.

Fish Riddle

[Alice] spoke to the Red Queen, whose answer was a little wide of the mark. "As to fishes," she said very slowly and solemnly, putting her mouth to Alice's ear, "her White Majesty knows a lovely riddle—all in poetry—all about fishes. Shall she repeat it?"

"Her Red Majesty's very kind to mention it," the White Queen murmured into Alice's other ear, in a voice like the cooing of a pigeon. "It would be *such* a treat! May I?"

"Please do," Alice said very politely.

The White Queen laughed with delight, and stroked Alice's cheek. Then she began:

> " 'First, the fish must be caught.'
> That is easy: a baby, I think could have caught it.
>   'Next, the fish must be bought.'
> That is easy: a penny, I think, would have bought it.
>
>   'Now cook me the fish!'
> That is easy, and will not take more than a minute.
>   'Let it lie in a dish!'
> That is easy, because it already is in it.
>
>   'Bring it here! Let me sup!'
> It is easy to set such a dish on the table.
>   'Take the dish-cover up!'
> Ah! *that* is so hard that I fear I'm unable!
>
>   For it holds it like glue—
> Holds the lid to the dish, while it lies in the middle:
>   Which is easiest to do,
> Un-dish-cover the fish, or dishcover the riddle?"

"Take a minute to think about it, and then guess," said the Red Queen. "Meanwhile we'll drink your health—Queen Alice's health!" she screamed at the top of her voice. . . .

This riddle comes from *Through the Looking-Glass* just after Alice reaches the far side of the chessboard in Chapter 9 and becomes Queen. Can you discover the fish-dish?

Cats and Rats

In the puzzle concerning the "Rule of Three" (number 8) a problem about "cats and rats" is included. It came from an article which Lewis Carroll contributed to a magazine called *The Monthly Packet* in February 1880. The article begins with a problem which has, in his view, four possible solutions depending on the interpretation of the original information. In all four cases, the consideration of fractional cats and rats is ruled out. The problem is as follows:

> If 6 cats kill 6 rats in 6 minutes, how many will be
> needed to kill 100 rats in 50 minutes?

Identify the four different ways in which the cats might kill the rats, and determine how many cats will be required in each scenario.

Syzygies

On 12 December 1879, Lewis Carroll wrote in his diary: "Invented a new way of working one word into another. I think of calling the puzzle *syzygies.*" He contributed the puzzle to *The Lady,* where it was published in July 1891. Two years later he reworked the puzzle and published it, together with a game called "Lanrick," in a stitched pamphlet that was, without doubt, created in preparation for his projected book "Original Games and Puzzles." This latter book was incomplete at the time of his death in 1898. Rules from the 1893 version of "Syzygies" are reproduced here.

1. DEFINITIONS

DEFINITION 1

When two words contain the same set of one or more consecutive letters, a copy of it, placed in a parenthesis between the two words, is called a 'Syzygy', and is said to 'yoke' one set to the other, and also to 'yoke' each letter of one set to the corresponding letter of the other set.
Examples to Def. 1

(1)	(2)	(3)	(4)
walrus	walrus	walrus	minc
(a)	(l)	(wa)	(mi)
swallow	swallow	swallow	mimic

N.B.—In Ex. (2), the Syzygy may be regarded as yoking the 'l' in 'walrus' to whichever 'l' in 'swallow' the writer may prefer. And in Ex. (4) the Syzygy may be regarded as yoking the 'mi' in 'mine' to whichever 'mi' in 'mimic' the writer may prefer.

DEFINITION 2

A set of four or more words, with a Syzygy between every two is called a 'Chain', of which all but the end-words are called 'Links'.

DEFINITION 3

In a 'Syzygy-Problem' two words are given, which are to form the end-words of a Chain.
Example to Def. 3

If the given words are 'walrus' and 'carpenter' (the Problem might be stated in the form *'Introduce* Walrus *to* Carpenter'), the following Chain would be a solution of the Problem:—

WALRUS
(rus)
peruse
(per)
harper
(arpe)
CARPENTER

DEFINITION 4

Every letter in a Chain, which is not yoked to some other, is called 'waste'; but, if either of the end-words contains more than 7 letters, the extra ones are not counted as waste.

Thus, in the above Chain, the 'wal' in 'walrus', the 'e' in 'peruse', the 'h' in 'harper', and the 'c' and the 'nter' in 'carpenter' are 'waste': so that this Chain has 10 waste letters; but since 2 of the 5 waste letters in 'carpenter' are not counted as waste, the Chain is reckoned as having only 8 waste letters. [Editor's note: "carpenter" contains 9 letters, which is 2 more than the 7 letters in a word specified by Carroll as being not counted.]

DEFINITION 5

When two words contain the same letter, but these two letters are forbidden to be yoked together, these two letters are said to be 'barred' with regard to each other.

2. RULES FOR MAKING CHAINS

RULE 1

A Chain should be written as in the Example to Def. 3. It does not matter which given word is placed at the top. Any number of alternative Chains may be sent in. [I.e., to *The Lady,* in response to the syzygies that Carroll created.—Editor's note.]

RULE 2

Any word, used as a Link, must satisfy all the following tests:—

(a) It may not be foreign, unless it is in such common use that it may fairly be regarded as naturalised. (The words 'ennui', 'minimum', 'nous', may be taken as specimens of words thus naturalised.)

(b) It must be in common use in conversation, letters, and books, in ordinary society. (Thus, slang words used only in particular localities, and words used only by specialists, are unlawful.)

(c) It may not be a proper name, when usually spelt with a capital letter. (Thus 'Chinese' is unlawful; but 'china', used as the name of a substance, is lawful.)

(d) It may not be an abbreviated or a compound word, when usually written with an apostrophe, or hyphen. (Thus, 'silver'd', 'don't', 'man's', 'coach-house', are unlawful.)

N.B.—If the Scorer accepts the infinitive of a verb as 'ordinary', he is bound to accept all its grammatical inflexions. Thus, if he accepts 'to strop (a razor)' as an ordinary word, he is bound to accept 'stroppest', 'stroppeth', 'stropping', and 'stropped', even though the first two have probably never been used by any human being.

But, if he accepts the singular of a noun as 'ordinary', he is not thereby bound to accept its plural; and *vice versa.*

Thus, he may accept 'remorse' and 'tidings' as 'ordinary', and yet reject 'remorses' and 'tiding' as 'non-ordinary'.

RULE 3

When two words begin with the same set of one or more consecutive letters, or would do so if certain prefixes were removed, each letter in the one set is 'barred' with regard to the corresponding letter in the other set.

Examples to Rule 3

Certain prefixes are here marked off by perpendicular lines, and the 'barred' letters are printed in italics.

(1)	(2)	(3)	(4)
*do*g	*car*riage	un| *do*ne	un| *do*ne
*do*or	*car*case	*do*or	in *do*ors

N.B.—The letters are only 'barred' as here marked. They may often be yoked in other ways: e.g., in Ex. (2), the 'ca' above may be yoked to the second 'ca' below.

RULE 4

When two words end with the same set of one or more consecutive letters, or would do so if certain suffixes were removed, each letter in the one set is 'barred' with regard to the corresponding letter in the other set.

Examples to Rule 4

Certain suffixes are here marked off by perpendicular lines, and the 'barred' letters are printed in italics.

(1)	(2)	(3)	(4)
me*at*	oni*on*	*sink*|ing	*sink*|ing
c*at*	mo*on*	*link*	*link*|s

(5)	(6)
infl*at*|ed	plu*ng*|es
sati*at*|ing	cha*ng*|ing

N.B.—The letters are only 'barred' as here marked. They may often be yoked in other ways: e.g., in Ex. (2), the first 'on' above may be yoked to the 'on' below: in Ex. (3), (4), the second 'in' above may be yoked to the 'in' below; in Ex. (5), the 'at' above may be yoked to the first 'at' below; and, in Ex. (6), the 'ng' above may be yoked to the second 'ng' below.

Observe that, in Ex. (5), the reason why 'at' is barred, is that the words become, when the suffixes are removed, 'inflate' and 'satiate', which end with the same 3 letters. Similarly in Ex. (6), 'plunge' and 'change' end with the same 3 letters. But in the words 'plunges' and 'singer', the 'ng' is not barred, since the words 'plunge' and 'sing' do not end with the same letters.

RULE 5

Nouns and verbs are not to be regarded as prefixes or suffixes. Thus 'landlord (and) handmade' would be a lawful Syzygy.

RULE 6

The letters 'i' and 'y' may be treated as if identical. Thus 'busy (usy) using' would be a lawful Syzygy.

RULE 7

The Score for a Chain may be calculated by writing down 7 numbers, as follows:—

(1) The greater No. of letters in an end-Syzygy, *plus* twice the least.

(2) The least No. of letters in a Syzygy.

(3) The sum of (1) *plus* the product of the two numbers next above (2).

(4) The No. of Links.

(5) The No. of waste letters.

(6) The sum of twice (4) plus (5).

(7) The remainder left after deducting (6) from (3). If (6) be greater than (3), the remainder is written as '0'.

No. (7) is entered as the Score of the Chain.

Example to Rule 7

The figures on the right indicate the Nos. of waste letters.

WALRUS	3
(rus)	
peruse	1
(per)	
harper	1
(arpe)	
CARPENTER	3

As the greatest No. of letters in an end-Syzygy is '4', and the least is '3', No. (1) is '10'. Also No. (2) is '3'. Hence No. (3) is the sum of '10' *plus* '4 times 5', i.e., it is '30'. Also there are 2 Links and 8 waste letters. Hence No. (4) is '2', No. (5) is '8'; and No. (6) is the sum of 'twice 2' *plus* '8'; i.e., it is '12'. Hence No. (7) is the remainder after deducting '12' from '30'; i.e., it is '18'; which is the Score for the Chain.

The result may be conveniently recorded thus:—

$$10, 3, 30; 2, 8, 12; 18$$

The formula for the Score may, for the benefit of Algebraists, be stated thus:—

Let a = greatest No. of letters in an end-Syzygy.

b = least [No. of letters in an end-Syzygy].

m = least No. in a Syzygy;

k = No. of Links;

w = No. of waste letters:

then the Score = $(a+2b)+(m+1)(m+2)-(2k+w)$.

3. RULES FOR SCORING CHAINS

RULE 1

If the writer of a Chain has omitted a Syzygy, the Scorer inserts a one-letter Syzygy, if he can find a lawful one.

RULE 2

If the writer has omitted a Link, the Scorer erases the two adjacent Syzygies, and proceeds as in Rule 1.

RULE 3

If a Link be mis-spelt, the Scorer corrects it.

RULE 4

If a Syzygy contains unlawful letters, the Scorer erases them, and deducts twice that number of marks from the Score.

RULE 5

If one of two consecutive Syzygies contains the other, the Scorer erases the intermediate Link, and one Syzygy containing the other.
Examples to Rule 5

	(1)	(2)
	meeting	meeting
	(ting)	(ting)
	tinge	tinge
	(ing)	(ting)
	loving	parting

N.B.—In Ex. (1) the Scorer erases 'tinge' and the first Syzygy: in Ex. (2), he erases 'tinge' and either Syzygy. The results are:—

	(1)	(2)
	meeting	meeting
	(ing)	(ting)
	loving	parting

both of which are, by Rule 4, unlawful Syzygies.

RULE 6

The penalty awarded by the preceding Rule, cannot be evaded by writing shorter Syzygies than might be claimed, so as to avoid the result of one containing the other. In such a case, the Scorer would treat them as if written in full.
Examples to Rule 6.

meeting
(tin)
tinge
(ng)
parting

This would be treated as if it had been written, in full.

RULE 7

If the Chain now contains less than two Links, or an unlawful Link or Syzygy, the Scorer rejects it. Otherwise he calculates its Score.

RULE 8

In reckoning 'the least number of letters in a Syzygy', the Scorer takes no notice of any Syzygies inserted by himself, unless there are no others.

RULE 9

If a writer sends in alternative Chains [i.e., to *The Lady*], the Scorer takes the best of them.

RULE 10

If all be rejected, the Scorer puts '0' against the writer's name, assigning a reason for rejecting each Chain.

RULE 11

In announcing a Problem [in the pages of *The Lady*], the Scorer may bar any word, that he likes to name, from being used as a Link. After receiving the 'First-Chains', he must publish a list of the Links which he regards as violating Rule 2, and of the Syzygies which he regards as violating, owing to the occurrence of prefixes or suffixes, Rule 3 or Rule 4, and he must then allow time for sending in 'Second-Chains.' He may not, when scoring, reject any 'First-Chain' for a defect which ought to have been, but was not, published in the above-named list.

Another example may help to make the scoring clearer:

COOK the DINNER

COOK
(coo)
scooping
(pin)
pinned
(inne)
DINNER

The waste letters are, in order, "1" for "k"; "2" for "s" and "g"; "1" for "d"; and "2" for "d" and "r"; making a total of "6."

$$a = 4, b = 3, m = 3, k = 2, w = 6$$

The Score is

$$(4+2\times3)+(3+1)(3+2)-(2\times2+6) = 20$$

Here are some Syzygies for you to work out; the scores to aim for are also given. Solutions are given at the end of the book.

Lay KNIFE by FORK	(21)
SPREAD the BANQUET	(27)
DEMAND a CORMORANT	(29)
Reconcile DOG to CAT	(19)

Pounds, Shillings and Pence

The following mathematical curiosity is recorded by Lewis Carroll's first biographer, his nephew, Stuart Dodgson Collingwood. He states that it was discovered, as far as he knows, by Lewis Carroll. It involves the old currency of the United Kingdom, and, for present-day readers, this reminder is included; 12 pence (d.) make a shilling (s.), and 20 shillings make a pound (£).

> Put down any number of pounds not more than twelve, any number of shillings under twenty, and any number of pence under twelve. Under the pounds put the number of pence, under the shillings the number of shillings, and under the pence the number of pounds, thus reversing the line.
> Subtract.
> Reverse the line again.
> Add.
> Answer, £12 18s. 11d., whatever numbers may have been selected.

Example: £9   15s.   7d.
             £7   15s.   9d. -
             ─────────────────
             £1   19s. 10d.
             £10 19s.   1d. +
             ─────────────────
             £12 18s. 11d.

Try this out with other amounts.
Find an algebraic proof for this result.

Three Triangles

During the last month of his life, Lewis Carroll was sent a mathematical problem from New York. Virtually the last entry in his diary, dated 19 December 1897, reads: "Sat up last night till 4 a.m., over a tempting problem, sent me from New York, to find three equal rational-sided right-angles triangles. I found two, whose sides are 20, 21, 29; 12, 35, 37; but could not find three."

By "equal triangles" he means triangles of "equal area" as demonstrated by his examples, both having an area of 210 square units.

With a little help from Pythagoras, find three triangles to meet the requirements given above.

Every Triangle Has a Pair of Equal Sides!

Lewis Carroll is credited with the following curious proof that every triangle has two equal sides; i.e. every triangle is isosceles. He probably intended to include this in his book of "Games and Puzzles" with the intention that the reader should find the fallacy. Can you discover the flaw in this proof?

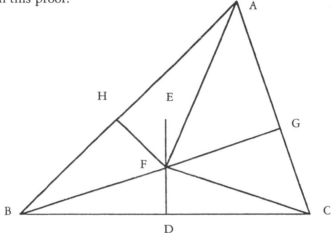

Let ABC be any Triangle. Bisect BC at D, and from D draw DE at right angles to BC. Bisect the angle BAC.

(1) If the bisector does not meet DE, they are parallel. Therefore AB = AC, i.e., ABC is isosceles.

(2) If the bisector meets DE, let them meet at F. Join FB, FC, and from F draw FG, FH, at right angles to AC, AB.

Then the Triangles AFG, AFH are equal, because they have the side AF common, and the angles FAG, AGF equal to FAH, AHF. Therefore AH = AG, and FH = FG.

Again, the Triangles BDF, CDF are equal, because BD = DC, DF is common, and the angles at D are equal. Therefore, FB = FC.

Again, the Triangles FHB, FGC are right-angled. Therefore the square on FB = the squares on FH, HB; and the square on FC = the squares on FG, GC. But FB = FC, and FH = FG. Therefore the square on HB = the square on GC. Therefore HB = GC. Also, AH has been proved = to AG. Therefore AB = AC; i.e., ABC is isosceles.

Therefore the Triangle ABC is always isosceles.

Q.E.D.

A Good Prospect

Lionel Tollemache, a scholar at Balliol College, Oxford, and the second son of the 1st Baron Tollemache, published an article in *Literature* dated 5 February 1898, titled "Reminiscences of Lewis Carroll." In it, he mentions a mathematical problem that Lewis Carroll proposed concerning the probability of tossing coins. The problem is as follows:

> Suppose that I toss up a coin on the condition that, if I throw heads once, I am to receive 1d.; if twice in succession, an additional dole of 2d.; if thrice, a further addition of 4d., and so on, doubling for each successful toss: what is the value of my prospects?

For example, he would win 3d. (three pennies) if he threw two heads in a row, but the chances of that happening are ½ for the first head and ½ for the second head; i.e., ¼ overall. Clearly, he wins more if he gets a long run of heads, but the chances of this happening diminishes as he throws each successive head. The problem is to work out his overall prospects.

The Telegraph Cipher

Lewis Carroll invented four different ciphers; the Telegraph Cipher was devised in April 1868. As with the Alphabet Cipher, which was explained in *Lewis Carroll's Games and Puzzles,* this cipher needs a "key-word." The original instructions for using the cipher are now at the Princeton University Library; they include a printed card with the alphabet printed twice, one above the other, separated by a thin line running horizontally as shown below:

KEY-ALPHABET

a b c d e f g h i j k l m n o p q r s t u v w x y z

---

a b c d e f g h i j k l m n o p q r s t u v w x y z a

MESSAGE-ALPHABET

The instructions for using the cipher are as follows:

1. Cut this card in two along the line.
2. In order to send messages in this cipher, a key-word must be agreed between the correspondents: this should be carried in the memory only.
3. To translate a message into cipher, write the key-word, letter for letter, over the message, repeating it as often as may be necessary: slide the message-cipher along under the other, so as to bring the first letter of the message under the first letter of the key-word, and copy the letter that stands over "a": then do the same with the second letter of the message and the second letter of the key-word, and so on.
4. Translate the cipher back into English by the same process.

In a letter to Edith Argles, sent soon after the cipher was invented, he demonstrated the method:

My dear Edith,
 I have tried my hand at a picture for you, but I have not much time for drawing, so it is but a simple affair. Also I enclose the new cipher; here is an example to make it clearer.

(key-word)	t r i c k t r i c k t r
(message)	c o m e t o m o r r o w
(cipher)	r d w y r f f u l t f v

Then translate back again,

(key-word)	t r i c k t r i c k t r
(cipher)	r d w y r f f u l t f v
(message)	c o m e t o m o r r o w

I enclose a key-word for Dolly [Edith's sister] to write with, if she likes. And I also send a bit of cipher for you and Dolly to amuse yourself by translating it. . . .

Here is a modified extract from a well-known book for you to decipher. The key-word is "forty-two":

Fdjru xwwzkyaqgq tbxt aqcsl rj zlfaobz nt muc egnvnc kg dhb nrgo, tjl rj ktdlji saymqgq vr ld. Arp pam lrv mttk yka oupl tbxt bnpszh. Wxqvpjdh o Vmqas Xfnqlf xovy zjgo pyknxrg wiiwb nt muc, eohgen ff ovnkgo,

"Km tkfx! Dm vpwx! X wktni vk mad iyas!" Vyk Atxsov madj y xwvdh dzf fr gmw vtqbdmroy-ekrmkm, oeq nfiebl ra qa, wbc vkpl mcxognqkg. Wdxmn myq jkkka suoixb wnpl t foenja cldh bgymuc w sfgzawfwv-qapjua ix f srawm da mohp kzd aa gy, bk bpk ooe twciwn vkp tlsdc omauc ov, fbo xyb nunv jg flkk ma zpu ld zrz ofcg w dfxlp htvnxv-kfnp cbcka arp pkcin.

30

Division by 9 and 11

On 27 September 1897, Lewis Carroll wrote in his diary that he had "discovered a rule for dividing a number by 9, by mere addition and subtraction. I felt sure there must be an analogous one for 11, and found it, and proved the first rule by Algebra, after working about nine hours!" The following day, he superseded his results by finding a method for determining the remainders after division by 9 and 11. These results were published in *Nature,* dated 14 October 1897. In essence, the method is as follows:

Suppose we wish to divide the number 2831 by 9.

First we find the remainder by adding up the digits; 2+8+3+1=14, and 1+4=5, and this is the remainder.

To find the quotient, we write the remainder 5 over the units-digit of 2831, and subtract; 5 minus 1 is 4. The figure 4 is written below the 1, and is the last digit in the answer. The figure 4 is also written above the 3 in the tens-column. Subtracting in the tens-column; 4 minus 3 is 1. The figure 1 is written below the 3, and is the tens-digit in the answer. The figure 1 is also written above the 8 in the hundreds-column. Subtracting in the hundreds-column; 1 minus 8, borrowing 10 from the thousands-column, is 3. The figure 3 is written below the 8 in the hundreds-column, and is the hundreds-digit in the answer. The figure 3 is also written above the 2 in the thousands-column, but since a number has previously been borrowed from this column, we change the number to 2. The subtraction is now complete. The calculation is illustrated below:

$$
\begin{array}{cccc}
3 & 1 & 4 & 5 \\
2 & 8 & 3 & 1 \\
\hline
 & 3 & 1 & 4 \\
\end{array}
\ -
$$

The answer is 314 with a remainder of 5.
Using this method, divide these numbers by 9:

(a) 1627 (b) 25073 (c) 513027 (d) 4180634

The division by 11 is similar. Suppose we wish to divide 2831 by 11.

First we find the remainder by adding up the alternate digits beginning with the units-figure. 1 plus 8 is 9. Then sum the remaining digits; 3 plus 2 is 5. Subtract the second result from the first; 9 minus 5, gives 4 which is the remainder.

To find the quotient, we now write the remainder *under* the units-digit of the original number, and subtract as before; 1 minus 4, borrowing 10 from the previous column, is 7. We write 7 under the 4, being the units-digit of the answer. We also write 7 under the 3 in the tens-column and subtract again remembering that a ten was borrowed, giving an answer of 5. This figure of 5 goes into the answer as the tens-digit. We also write 5 under the 8 in the hundreds-column and subtract remembering that a ten was borrowed last time, giving an answer of 2. This figure of 2 goes into the answer as the hundreds-column. We also write 2 under the 2 in the thousands-column and subtract giving zero. The subtraction is complete. The calculation is illustrated below:

$$
\begin{array}{r}
2\ 8\ 3\ 1 \\
2\ 5\ 7\ 4\ - \\
\hline
2\ 5\ 7
\end{array}
$$

The answer is 257 with a remainder of 4.

Using this method, divide these numbers by 11:

(a) 2517   (b) 32871   (c) 814924   (d) 6067895

"Can you do Addition?" the White Queen asked. "What's one and one and one and one and one and one and one and one and one and one?"

"I don't know," said Alice. "I lost count."

"She ca'n't do Addition," the Red Queen interrupted. "Can you do Subtraction? Take nine from eight."

"Nine from eight, I ca'n't, you know," Alice replied very readily: "but . . ."

"She ca'n't do Subtraction," said the White Queen. "Can you do Division? Divide a loaf by a knife—what's the answer to *that*?"

"I suppose——" Alice was beginning, but the Red Queen answered for her. "Bread-and-butter, of course."

Coins

This original problem by Lewis Carroll involves coins from the old currency; by way of reminder, a pound is 20 shillings (s.), and a shilling is 12 pence (d.). A half-sovereign is 10 shillings, a crown is 5 shillings, a double-florin is 4 shillings, a half-crown is 2 shillings and sixpence, a florin is 2 shillings. The problem is as follows:

A man who possesses a half-sovereign, a florin and a sixpence goes into a shop and buys goods worth 7 shillings and 3 pence. But the shopkeeper cannot give him the correct change, as his coins are a crown, a shilling, and a penny. But a friend comes into the shop, and finds that he has a double-florin, a half-crown, a fourpenny piece and a threepenny bit.

Can the shopkeeper effect an exchange that will enable him to give the man the correct change, and to give his friend the exact equivalent of his coins?

Bag Containing Tickets

A slip of paper in Lewis Carroll's handwriting was discovered among some papers belonging to Professor Bartholomew Price, his mathematics tutor. The paper, containing a probability problem, is reproduced in facsimile below. This is the first time that the problem has been published.

A bag contains 12 tickets, 3 marked 'A', 4 'B', 5 'C'. One is drawn in the presence of 12 witnesses of equal credibility: three say it was 'A', four 'B', five 'C'. What is the chance that it was 'A'?

A bag contains 12 tickets, 3 marked 'A'; 4 'B', 5 'C'. One is drawn in the presence of 12 witnesses of equal credibility: three say it was 'A', four 'B', five 'C'. What is the chance that it was 'A'?

33

Going to the Theatre

Lewis Carroll was very fond of going to the theatre. He was also a good dinner-table host, and often entertained guests with problems and conundrums with a mathematical flavour. One particular guest who recorded some of these puzzles was Viscount Simon, an undergraduate at Wadham College, Oxford, and later Fellow of All Souls. He remembered a problem concerning a theatre trip:

> A man wanted to go to the theatre, which would cost him 1 shilling and 6 pence, but he only had a shilling. So he went to a Pawnbroker's shop and offered to pledge his shilling for a loan. The Pawnbroker satisfied himself that the shilling was genuine and lent him 9 pence on it.
> The man then came out of the shop with 9 pence and the Pawnbroker's ticket for 1 shilling. Outside he met a friend to whom he offered to sell the Pawnbroker's ticket and the friend bought it from him for 9 pence. He now had 9 pence from the Pawnbroker and another 9 pence from the friend and so was able to go to the theatre.

The question posed by Lewis Carroll was, "Who lost what?"

Two Tumblers

Another puzzle remembered and recorded by Viscount Simon concerned two tumblers.

Take two tumblers, one of which contains 50 spoonfuls of pure brandy and the other 50 spoonfuls of pure water. Take from the first of these one spoonful of brandy and transfer it without spilling into the second tumbler and stir it up. Then take a spoonful of the mixture and transfer it back without spilling to the first tumbler.

Lewis Carroll's question was, "If you consider the whole transaction, has more brandy been transferred from the first tumbler to the second, or more water from the second to the first?"

35

Roman Numerals

A puzzle that was circulating around Oxford in 1888, and one that Lewis Carroll almost certainly came across, concerned Roman numerals. A copy of the problem was found with other papers in the collection of Professor Bartholomew Price, Lewis Carroll's mathematics tutor and lifelong friend and colleague. Many of these scraps of paper are in Lewis Carroll's handwriting; this one is not, so it is likely that he did not invent the problem.

> Reader, whether man or woman
> Write my age in figures Roman
> Three lettered units then you'll find
> Each of them different in kind;
> The first divided by the second
> Will give the third, if rightly reckoned
> Ten times the whole will let you see
> My University degree.

Spheres and Dodecahedrons

This problem comes from a letter, reproduced below in facsimile, written by Lewis Carroll to his old mathematics tutor, Professor Bartholomew Price, who was then Master of Pembroke College, Oxford.

The problem is about filling space with spheres. Lewis Carroll suggests that the space remaining could be taken up by enclosing each sphere in a dodecahedron, a twelve-sided shape with pentagonal faces. The question is whether the dodecahedrons would fit together and leave no gaps, and whether the pentagonal faces would be regular; i.e., have five sides of equal length. What do you think?

Ch. Ch. May 18/97

Dear Master,

Am I right in thinking that space could be filled (barring certain interstices) with equal spheres, each touching 12 others? If so, & if all the tangent-planes were produced till they intersected other tangent-planes, should we not exhaust the interstices, & fill space with plane-sided dodecahedra? And if so, would these dodecahedra have the usual pentagonal facets?

Sincerely yours
C. L. Dodgson.

Predicting the Total

Many people have recorded their reminiscences of Lewis Carroll. Lancelot Robson published his memories in the *Reader's Digest* in February 1953. He wrote:

> One day we were having a children's party and unexpectedly "Mr. Alice in Wonderland", as we called him, came in to see my father. How delighted we were! He asked us if, at our school, we did sums. A chorus answered, "Yes." There was a pause, then Lewis Carroll said, "I am afraid you go to a very poor school. I never do sums; I always put the answer down first and set the sum afterwards."
> There was silence.
> Then he continued, "We will do some sums." He wrote some figures on a piece of paper, and gave it to my stepmother, saying, "That will be the answer to our sum when we have set it."

The answer he probably wrote on the piece of paper was 21,064. This is how the conundrum proceeds.

He asks the assembled audience for a well-known date in history, getting, without much doubt, 1066. This he writes down as the start of the sum. He then gets members of the audience to give him numbers of their own choosing to form another four-digit number, say for example: 2948. This would be written under 1066. Without any hesitation he would add 7051. Then he would ask for another four-digit number, say 5651, to which he would add, again almost instantaneously, 4348. The sum would now look like this:

```
    1 0 6 6     date chosen by audience
    2 9 4 8     numbers chosen by audience
    7 0 5 1     Lewis Carroll's numbers
    5 6 5 1     numbers chosen by audience
    4 3 4 8  +  Lewis Carroll's numbers
  2 1 0 6 4
```

The answer is exactly as he had predicted.

How is it done? How did Lewis Carroll know, in an instant, what numbers he should write down?

The Impossible Hole

Another party trick that Lewis Carroll performed concerned two coins, a sixpence and a half-penny. Readers will remember that a sixpence is smaller in size than a half-penny.

The relative sizes are illustrated here:

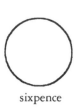

sixpence

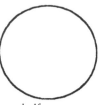

half-penny

Lewis Carroll would draw round the sixpence on a piece of paper, and then cut out the circular hole so that it was exactly the size of the sixpenny coin. He would then pose the question: "Can you put the ha'penny through it?"

Seems impossible, but there is a way. How does the ha'penny go through the smaller hole?

Excelsior

In 1885, Lewis Carroll published a book that he called *A Tangled Tale*. It contained a series of mathematical puzzles, or "knots" as he called them, bound together by a narrative story about a family. The knots had originally been published in *The Monthly Packet*, a magazine chiefly for young ladies, edited by Charlotte Yonge. This puzzle about the path of two knights, which had appeared in *The Monthly Packet* in 1880 as the first knot, became the first chapter in *A Tangled Tale*.

The problem is about two knights, one young, one much older, descending a mountainside at six miles per hour. As they proceed, the younger knight speaks:

"A goodly pace, I trow!" he exclaimed. "We sped not thus in the ascent!"

"Goodly, indeed!" the other echoed with a groan. "We clomb it but at three miles in the hour."

"And on the dead level our pace is ——?" the younger suggested; for he was weak in statistics, and left all such details to his aged companion.

"Four miles in the hour," the other wearily replied. "Not an ounce more," he added, with that love of metaphor so common in old age, "and not a farthing less!"

"'Twas three hours past high noon when we left our hostelry," the young man said, musingly.

The story continues and it transpires that it will be nine o'clock before they return to their hostelry. The question is, how many miles will they have trudged along the level road and up the hill and then back home again? A supplementary question is, within half an hour, at what time did they reach the top of the hill?

Eligible Apartments

In the second chapter of *A Tangled Tale,* a tutor and his two scholars, Hugh and Lambert, are looking for lodgings. They come across a square in the town that has four houses displaying cards which say "Eligible Apartments." However, only single rooms are to be had. There are 20 houses on each side of the square, the doors of which divide the side into 21 equal parts. The houses with the available lodgings are at numbers 9, 25, 52 and 73. The tutor decides to make one of the rooms a "day-room" and take the rest as bedrooms. He sets this problem for his scholars:

"One day-room and three bed-rooms. . . . We will take as our day-room the one that gives us the least walking to do to get to it."
"Must we walk from door to door, and count the steps?" said Lambert.
"No, no! Figure it out, my boys, figure it out!"

Hence, with the provision that it is possible to cross the square directly from door to door, which house will be used for the day-room?

Who's Coming to Dinner?

In the same chapter of *A Tangled Tale*, Hugh and Lambert have received a letter from their father from abroad, over which they have been puzzling. It concerns the Governor of Kgovjni, their father's friend, who is organising a dinner-party. The problem is this:

"Well, yes. The Governor of——what-you-may-call-it——wants to give a *very* small dinner-party, and he means to ask his father's brother-in-law, his brother's father-in-law, his father-in-law's brother, and his brother-in-law's father: and we're to guess how many guests there will be."

How many dinner guests will there be if the size of the party is to be minimised?

42

Memoria Technica

Lewis Carroll had a very good memory, except for faces and dates, the former giving him some very embarrassing moments. To help himself remember dates and numbers, he devised a system of verse-mnemonics that he circulated among his friends. In his diary for 1 June 1877, he recorded: "The new 'Memoria Technica' works beautifully. I made rhymes for the foundations of all the Colleges (except Univ.). At night I made lines giving pi to 71 decimal places." This is his system:

My "Memoria Technica" is a modification of Gray's; but, whereas he used both consonants and vowels to represent digits, and had to content himself with a syllable of gibberish to represent the date or whatever other number was required, I use only consonants, and fill in with vowels *ad libitum*, and thus can always manage to make a real word of whatever has to be represented.

The principles on which the necessary 20 consonants have been chosen are as follows:

1. "b" and "c," the first two consonants in the alphabet.
2. "d" from "duo," "w" from "two."
3. "t" from "tres," the other may wait awhile.
4. "f" from "four," "q" from "quattuor."
5. "l" and "v," because "l" and "v" are the Roman symbols for "fifty and "five."
6. "s" and "x" from "six."
7. "p" and "m" from "septem."
8. "h" from "huit," and "k" from the Greek "okto."
9. "n" from "nine"; and "g" because it is so like a "9."
0. "z" and "r" from "zero."

There is now one consonant still waiting for its digit, viz., "j," and one digit waiting for its consonant, viz., "3," the conclusion is obvious.

The result may be tabulated thus:

1	2	3	4	5	6	7	8	9	0
b	d	t	f	l	s	p	h	n	z
c	w	j	q	v	x	m	k	g	r

When a word has been found, whose last consonants represent the number required, the best plan is to put it as the last word of a rhymed couplet, so that, whatever other words in it are forgotten, the rhyme will secure the only really important word.

Now suppose you wish to remember the date of the discovery of America, which is 1492; the "1" may be left out as obvious; all we need is "492."

Write it thus:

$$\begin{array}{ccc} 4 & 9 & 2 \\ f & n & d \\ q & g & w \end{array}$$

and try to find a word that contains "f" or "q," "n" or "g," "d" or "w." A word soon suggests itself—"found."

The poetic faculty must now be brought into play, and the following couplet will soon be evolved:

> "Columbus sailed the world around,
> Until America was FOUND."

If posible, invent the couplets for yourself; you will remember them better than any others.

The following couplets identify the dates specified; can you find required dates using the Memoria Technica outlined above?

The foundation of Brasenose College:

> With a nose that is brazen
> Our gate we EMBLAZON.

The foundation of St. John's College, with its splendid lawns:

> They must have a bevel
> To keep them so LEVEL.

Finally, the foundation of Lewis Carroll's own College, Christ Church:

> Ring Tom when you please:
> We ask but SMALL FEES.

This is probably a reference to the sub-committee of the Governing Body at Christ Church, who determined that those people who wished to strike the bell in Tom Tower, a frequent treat for Lewis Carroll's young guests, would have to pay a fee of 2d. for the privilege.

THE SOLUTIONS
TO THE PUZZLES

1. *Why Is a Raven Like a Writing-Desk?*

Lewis Carroll gave his own solution to the problem in the original version of the "Preface to the Eighty-Sixth Thousand" of *Alice's Adventures in Wonderland,* in which he wrote:

> Enquiries have been so often addressed to me, as to whether any answer to the Hatter's Riddle . . . can be imagined, that I may as well put on record here what seems to me to be a fairly appropriate answer, viz. "Because it can produce a few notes, though they are *very* flat; and it is nevar put with the wrong end in front!" This, however, is merely an after-thought: the Riddle, as originally invented, had no answer at all.

Notice the spelling of "never" in this extract, which reverses very smartly to give "raven"! Other suggestions have been:

> Because Poe wrote on both [Sam Loyd].
> Because it slopes with a flap [Cyril Pearson].
> Because there is a "b" in both [E. V. Rieu].
> Because both have quills dipped in ink [David Jodrey].
> Because both have two eyes [Izumi Yasui].

2. *A Rebus Letter*

The letter was written from the home of Lewis Carroll's sisters in Guildford, called "The Chestnuts."

The Chestnuts

My dear Ina,

Though I don't give birthday *presents,* still I may write a birthday letter. I came to your door to wish you many happy returns of the day, but the cat met me, and took me for a mouse, and hunted me up and down till I could hardly stand. However *some*how I got into the house, and there a mouse met me, and took me for a cat, and pelted me with fire-irons, pots and pans, and wine-bottles. Of course I ran into the street again, and a horse met me and took me for a cart, and dragged me all the way to the Guildhall,* but the worst of all was when a cart met me and took me for a horse. I was harnessed to it, and had to draw it miles and miles, all the way to Merrow. So you see I couldn't get to the room where you were.

However I was glad to hear you were hard at work learning the multiplication tables for a birthday treat.

*This might be interpreted as "station" but for the fact that the Guildhall in the centre of Guildford has a clock on a beam as shown in the picture, and Ina would have known this landmark well.

I had just time to look into the kitchen, and saw your birthday feast getting ready, a nice bowl of crusts, bones, pills, cotton-bobbins, and rhubarb and magnesia. "Now," I thought, "she will be happy!" and with a smile I went on my way.

Your aff[ectiona]te friend
CLD

3. A Spiral Letter

Why, how *can* she know that no harm has come to it? Surely *I* must know best, having the book before me from morning to night, and gazing at it *for hours together* with tear-dimmed eyes? Why, there were several things I didn't even mention, for instance, the number of beetles that had got crushed between the leaves. So when *I* sign myself 'your loving' *you* go down a step, & say 'your affectionate'? Very well, then *I* go down *another* step, and sign myself 'yours truly, Lewis Carroll.' Oct[ober] 22/ [18]78.

4. The Captive Queen

Since the baskets are of equal weight, we can assume that they exactly counterbalance each other halfway between the ground and the window. First, one of the baskets is pulled up to the window. The following table will indicate the order in which the family make their way to the ground. On some occasions, the weights in both baskets are equal, and it may be assumed that, by pulling on the ropes, it is possible to make the appropriate basket reach the ground.

Key: Q, Queen; D, Daughter; S, Son; and W, Weight.

Window level:	QDSW	QDS	QD W	QD	Q SW
Ground level:		W	S	SW	D

Q S	Q W	DS	D W	D	SW
D W	DS	Q W	Q S	Q SW	QD

S	W
QD W	QDS

Additional problem:

Key: as above, and p, pig; d, dog; c, cat.

Window level:	QDSpdcW	QDSpdc	QD pdcW	QD pdc
Ground level:		W	S	S W

QD d W	QD cW	QD c	Q S cW	Q S c	Q c W
Sp c	Spd	Spd W	D pd	D pd W	DSpd

DS c	Q S	Q	W DS	D	W D
Q pd W	D pdcW	DSpdc	Q pdcW	Q Spdc	Q SpdcW

```
   S    W        S                       W
QD  pdc      QD  pdcW         QDSpdc
```

5. *A New Way to Pay Old Debts*

The bill had doubled each year for six years.

    (a) £2,048,000   (b) £2,097,152,000   (c) £2,147,483,648,000

The 64th square will contain (if there is sufficient room!) almost £92,233,720,368,548,000.

6. *The Day of the Week for Any Given Date*

    (a) Saturday   (b) Sunday   (c) Friday
    (d) Friday   (e) Wednesday   (f) Tuesday

7. *A Geometrical Paradox*

In the second 5 × 13 diagram, the diagonal is not a straight line, but is a slightly hollow quadrilateral with an area of one square.

8. *The Rule of Three*

A "mathematical" answer might be 5.76 seconds (assuming that the working day is 24 hours long!), but this is all nonsense. As Lewis Carroll pointed out to his students, most of the men would not get anywhere near the wall! The building area would be too cramped.

Lewis Carroll put forward the notion that the rats would more than likely kill the cat!

9. *The Monkey and Weight Problem*

Lewis Carroll gave his own solution to the problem in a letter to Professor Price in which he states that, in his opinion, the "weight" goes neither up nor down. However, the opinion of most mathematicians and scientists today is that the weight and monkey would always remain opposite to each other; hence, as the monkey climbs up the rope, the weight also goes up.

10. *Crossing the River*

Code the four gentlemen and their wives as follows: M1, W1; M2, W2; M3, W3; M4 and W4. A possible solution is as follows:

1st crossing:	M1 and W1 cross; M1 returns
2nd crossing:	M2 and W2 cross; M2 returns
3rd crossing:	M1 and M2 cross; M2 and W2 return
4th crossing:	W2 and W3 cross; M1 returns
5th crossing:	M1 and M2 cross; W3 returns
6th crossing:	M3 and M4 cross; M3 returns
7th crossing:	M3 and W3 cross; M4 returns
8th crossing:	M4 and W4 cross

12. More Doublets

BAT	TEA	CAR	MUM		
m a t	p e a	c a n	d u m		
MAN	p e t	VAN	d u d or dam		
	POT		DAD		

JOE	TILES	STALK	HOAX	JACK	DINNER
d o e	t i l l s	s t a l e	c o a x	s a c k	s i n n e r
d i e	t e l l s	s t a r e	c o a l	s i c k	s i n g e r
d i d	s e l l s	s c a r e	c o o l	s i l k	l i n g e r
a i d	s e a l s	s c o r e	FOOL	s i l l	l o n g e r
a n d	s e a r s	s c o r n		JILL	c o n g e r
ANN	s t a r s	ACORN			c o n f e r
	s t a r e				c o f f e r
	s t a t e				COFFEE
	SLATE				

BOAT	NOUN	SHIP	PLANT	UNIT	LIES
b o l t	n o o n	s l i p	p l a n s	k n i t	l e e s
b o l d	m o o n	s l a p	p l a t s	k n o t	f e e s
b a l d	m o r n	s o a p	p e a t s	k n o b	f e e t
b a r d	m o r e	s o a k	b e a t s	s n o b	f r e t
b a r s	m e r e	s o c k	BEANS	s n u b	f r e e
OARS	h e r e	DOCK		s n u g	t r e e
	h e r b			s l u g	TRUE
	VERB			s l u r	
				s o u r	
				FOUR	

HORSE	OPEN	CRY	BOWLER
h o u s e	o v e n	c o y	b o w l e d
r o u s e	e v e n	c o t	c o w l e d
r o u t e	e v e s	c u t	c o o l e d
r o u t s	e y e s	OUT	c o o k e d
b o u t s	d y e s		l o o k e d
b o a t s	d o e s		l o c k e d
b r a t s	d o t s		l i c k e d
b r a s s	d o t e		w i c k e d
GRASS	d a t e		WICKET
	GATE		

13. Names in Poems

The names are identified by the first letter in each line: LORINA, ALICE and EDITH.

The name is revealed by taking the second letter in each line: EDITH RIX.

Again, the first letter in each line reveals their names: MINNIE, ELLA and EMMIE.

14. *Anagrams*

Florence Nightingale.

15. *The Flower Riddle*

Lion's-tooth, Ox-eye, Cat's-foot, Fox-tail Grass, Mouse-ear Chickweed, Hound's-tongue, Goats'-beard and Maidenhair are all names of wildflowers or grasses.

16. *Feeding the Cat*

The solution to this and the next puzzle were printed in *Aunt Judy's Magazine* in January 1871; the answers were given in poems written by "Eadgyth."

> That salmon and sole Puss should think very grand
>   Is no such remarkable thing.
> For more of these dainties Puss took up her stand;
> But when the third sister stretched out her fair hand
>   Pray why should Puss swallow her ring?

17. *The Sun and the Moon*

> "In these degenerate days," we oft hear said,
>   "Manners are lost and chivalry is dead!"
> No wonder, since in high exalted spheres
>   The same degeneracy, in fact, appears.
> The Moon, in social matters interfering,
>   Scolded the Sun, when early in appearing;
> And the rude Sun, her gentle sex ignoring,
>   Called her a fool, thus her pretensions flooring.

("Full" being heard as "fool").

18. *Tangrams*

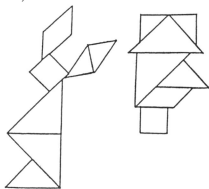

19. *A Sticky but Polished Riddle*

The first is "co"; an obbreviation of "company."
The second is "pal"; a jolly friend.
The whole is "copal"; a resin used for making varnish.

20. *Anagrammatic Sonnet*

As to:	OATS or STOA
the war:	WREATH
try elm:	TERMLY or MYRTLE
I tried:	TIDIER
The wig:	WEIGHT
cast in:	ANTICS or SCIANT
I went:	TWINE
to ride:	RIOTED
Ring? Yes:	SYRINGE
We rang:	GNAWER
Let's rap:	PLASTER
We don't:	WONTED
O shew:	WHOSE
her wit!:	WHITER or WITHER
As yet:	YEAST
she won't:	SOWNETH or HOT-NEWS or NEW-SHOT
Saw eel:	WEASEL
in Rome:	MERINO or MOIREN
Dry one:	YONDER
he's wet:	THEWES
I am dry:	MYRIAD
O forge!:	FOREGO
Th'rogue:	ROUGETH
Why a net?:	HAY WENT or WAY THEN

Some of these words are rather obscure; perhaps you can find better alternatives.

The compound word from "abcdefgi" is "big-faced." The connection with "summer-house" must have been an in-joke, now lost on us.

21. *A Charade*

The first is "sea"; the second is "son"; the whole "season."

22. *Fish Riddle*

A solution to this riddle appeared in the October 1878 issue of a magazine called *Fun*. It was included in a poem that had been submitted by an anonymous reader and then was slightly amended by Lewis Carroll before publication:

> First pull up the fish.
> It can't swim away: for a fish this is funny!
> Next 'tis bought; and I wish
> That a penny was always adequate money.

Make it ready to eat—
Fetching pepper and vinegar won't take a minute.
   Dish with cover complete,
Of lovely shell china, already 'tis in it.

   Now 'tis time we should sup.
What's one only, you dolt? Set a score on the table!
   Take the dish-cover up—
With mere finger and thumb you will never be able.

   Get an oyster-knife strong,
Insert it 'twixt cover and dish, in the middle;
   Then you shall before long
Un-dish-cover the OYSTERS—dishcover the riddle!

23. *Cats and Rats*

Lewis Carroll's own solution is reproduced here:

This is a good example of a phenomenon that often occurs in working problems in double proportion; the answer looks all right at first, but, when we come to test it, we find that, owing to peculiar circumstances in the case, the solution is either impossible or else indefinite, and needing further data. The "peculiar circumstance" here is that fractional cats or rats are excluded from consideration, and in consequence of this the solution is, as we shall see, indefinite.

The solution, by ordinary rules of Double Proportion, is as follows:

$$6 \text{ rats} : 100 \text{ rats} \ \& \ 50 \text{ min} : 6 \text{ min} :: 6 \text{ cats} : \text{answer}$$

$$\text{therefore} \qquad \text{answer} = \frac{100 \times 6 \times 6}{6 \times 50} = 12$$

But when we come to trace the history of this sanguinary scene through all its horrid details, we find that at the end of 48 minutes 96 rats are dead and that there remain 4 live rats and 2 minutes to kill them in: the question is, can this be done?

Now there are at least *four* different ways in which the original feat of 6 cats killing 6 rats in 6 minutes, may be achieved. For the sake of clearness let us tabulate them:

A. All 6 cats are needed to kill a rat; and this they do in one minute, the other rats standing meekly by, waiting their turn.

B. 3 cats are needed to kill a rat, and they do it in 2 minutes.

C. 2 cats are needed, and they do it in 3 minutes.

D. Each cat kills a rat all by itself, and takes 6 minutes to do it.

In cases A and B it is clear that the 12 cats (who are assumed to come quite fresh from their 48 minutes of slaughter) can finish the affair in the required time; but, in case C, it can only be done by supposing that 2 cats could kill two-thirds of a rat in 2 minutes; and in case D, by supposing that a cat could kill one-third of a rat in 2 minutes. Neither supposition is warranted by the data; nor could the fractional rats (even if endowed with equal vitality) be fairly assigned to the different cats. For my part, if I were a cat in case D, and did not find my claws in good working order, I should certainly prefer to have my one-third-rat cut off from the tail end.

In cases C and D, then, it is clear that we must provide extra cat-power. In case C *less* than 2 extra cats would be of no use. If 2 were supplied, and if they began killing their 4 rats at the beginning of the time, they would finish them in 12 minutes, and have 36 minutes to spare, during which they might weep, like Alexander, because there were not 12 more rats to kill. In case D, one extra cat would suffice; it would kill its 4 rats in 24 minutes, and have 24 minutes to spare, during which it could have killed another 4. But in neither case could any use be made of the last 2 minutes, except to half-kill rats—a barbarity we need not take into consideration.

To sum up our results. If the 6 cats kill the 6 rats by method A or B, the answer is "12"; if by method C, "14"; if by method D, "13."

This, then, is an instance of a solution made "indefinite" by the circumstances of the case.

24. *Syzygies*

Scores are given below each syzygy:

KNIFE
(nife)
manifest
(man)
workman
(ork)
FORK

10,3,30;2,5,9:21

SPREAD
(read)
readiness
(ines)
shines
(shin)
vanquishing
(anqu)
BANQUET

12,4,42;3,9,15:27

DEMAND
(eman)
gentleman
(gent)
tangent
(ange)
orange
(oran)
CORMORANT

12,4,42;3,7,13:29

DOG
(dog)
endogen
(gen)
gentry
(ntry)
intricate
(cat)
CAT

9,3,29;3,4,10:19

25. *Pounds, Shillings and Pence*

£	s.	d.
x	y	z
z	y	x −
(x − z − 1)	19	(12 + z − x)
(12 + z − x)	19	(x − z − 1) +
12	18	11

26. *Three Triangles*

The three smallest equal rational-sided right-angled triangles have sides of lengths: 40, 42, 58; 24, 70, 74; 15, 112, 113. The area of each is 840 square units.

The general solution of the problem is:

(i)	$a = 2mn$	$b = m^2 - n^2$	$c = m^2 + n^2$
(ii)	$a = mk$	$b = m^2 - k^2$	$c = m^2 + k^2$
(iii)	$a = 2m(n + k)$	$b = (n + k)^2 - m^2$	$c = (n + k)^2 + m^2$

$$\text{where } k = 2p + 1, m = p^2 + p + 1, n = p^2 - 1$$

The solution given above is found by taking $p = 2$.

27. *Every Triangle Has a Pair of Equal Sides!*

If you are having difficulty in finding the fallacy in the proof, try drawing an accurate diagram of the triangle and the other lines which are indicated.

28. *A Good Prospect*

The probability of getting the first head is ½, for which he earns 1d. (one penny). The probability of getting the second head is ¼, for which he earns an extra 2d. The probability of getting the third head is ⅛, for which he earns an extra 4d. And so on. Thus, his prospects are (½ times 1d.) plus (¼ times 2d.) plus (⅛ times 4d.), and so on. Each of these terms equals ½d. Hence, his prospects are ½d. for every successive throw of a head.

29. *The Telegraph Cipher*

Decoding the text gives the following:

Alice was getting very tired of sitting by her sister on the bank, and having nothing to do. The hot day made her feel very sleepy. Suddenly a White Rabbit with pink eyes ran close by her, saying to itself,

"Oh dear! Oh dear! I shall be too late!" The Rabbit took a watch out of its waistcoat-pocket, and looked at it, and then hurried on. Alice had never before seen a rabbit with either a waistcoat-pocket or a watch to take out of it, so she ran across the field after it, and was just in time to see it pop down a large rabbit-hole under the hedge.

31. *Coins*

If all the money is pooled, the following coins are at hand:

10s., 5s., 4s., 2/6 (2s. and 6d.), 2s., 1s., 6d., 4d., 3d. and 1d.

The man needs 5/3 change for his purchases; hence, he gets 5s. and 3d.

The friend loans 7/1; hence, he gets 4s., 2/6, 6d. and 1d.

The shopkeeper should now have his original cash, 6/1, and the cost of the sales, 7/3; i.e., 13/4. He gets the remaining coins, 10s., 2s., 1s. and 4d. and everyone is happy.

32. *Bag Containing Tickets*

Let the credibility of a witness be "a" when telling the truth. Hence, the credibility of a witness when telling a lie is "1 - a."

If it was A, then 3 tell the truth, and 9 lie; hence the credibility is 3 in 12, or 1 in 4.

Therefore, the chance that it is A, and no other, is:

$$3/12 \times 1/4 + 4/12 \times 3/4 + 5/12 \times 3/4 = 5/8$$

33. *Going to the Theatre*

Viscount Simon recalled the conversation resulting from this conundrum. He offered the answer that the friend lost 6d. as he had to repay the loan to the Pawnbroker in order to recover the shilling. He reports that Lewis Carroll said to him: "My young friend, your answer is not indeed right, but it does you the greatest credit, for it shows that you are so ignorant in the ways of Pawnbrokers that you think they do their business for nothing!" The Pawnbroker's charge had not been added on.

34. *Two Tumblers*

Most people go for the first suggestion, since a spoonful of pure brandy was placed in the second tumbler, while only a mixture of brandy and water was taken back.

In fact, both suggestions are wrong. Since the tumblers were originally filled to the same level, they will again be equally full after the two transactions. The volume of brandy now missing from the first tumbler has been replaced by water from the second tumbler. Similarly, the amount of water missing from the second tumbler has been replaced by brandy from the first tumbler. The amount of brandy or water transferred is the same in each case.

35. *Roman Numerals*

LXV or 65. 10 times 65 is 650 or DCL (Doctor of Civil Law).

36. *Spheres and Dodecahedrons*

Lewis Carroll is wrong in thinking that it takes 12 equal spheres to totally surround another. Hence, dodecahedrons would not solve the problem.

37. *Predicting the Total*

You may have spotted that any digit written by Lewis Carroll underneath a number written by the audience totals to 9. Hence, the original figure of 1066 has been increased by two amounts of 9999. Anticipating the date of 1066, Lewis Carroll added 20,000 less 2, giving 21064, which is the number he wrote on the piece of paper before the audience were invited to make up the sum.

The trick is easily repeated, if you know the age of one of the audience. Write that person's year of birth, plus 30,000 less 3, on a piece of paper. Invite the person to give you his or her year of birth. Repeat the construction of the sum as above, adding two extra lines. He will be just as surprised when you reveal that you knew the answer from the outset.

38. *The Impossible Hole*

Fold the piece of paper so that the crease forms the diameter of the hole that is the size of the six-penny piece. Place the half-penny in the hole so that it drops slightly through along the crease. If you gently bend the piece of paper so that the crease gradually curves, the half-penny will easily drop through.

39. *Excelsior*

Twenty-four miles; half-past six.

A level mile takes a quarter of an hour, uphill one-third, downhill one-sixth. Hence to go and return over the same mile, whether on the level or on the hillside, takes half an hour. Hence in six hours they went twelve miles out and twelve back. If the twelve miles out had been nearly all level, they would have taken a little over three hours; if nearly all uphill, a little under four. Hence three and a half hours must be within half an hour of the time taken in reaching the peak; thus, as they started at three, they got there within half an hour of half past six.

40. *Eligible Apartments*

The day-room is number 9.

Let A be No. 9, B be No. 25, C be No. 52 and D be No. 73. By the theorem of Pythagoras, it will be determined that the distances between the rooms are as follows:

$$AB = 13, AC = 21, AD = 12+ \text{ (between 12 and 13)}$$
$$BC = 20, BD = 21+, CD = 15+$$

Hence the sum of the distances from A is between 46 and 47; from B, between 54 and 55; from C, between 56 and 57; from D, between 48 and 51. Hence the sum is least for A.

41. *Who's Coming to Dinner?*

There is only one guest.

In this genealogy, males are denoted by capitals, and females by small letters. The Governor is E and his guest is C.

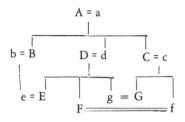

42. *Memoria Technica*

The foundation of Brasenose is dated 1509.
The foundation of St. John's is dated 1555.
The foundation of Christ Church is dated 1546.

Sources

The Tutor's Assistant; Being a Compendium of Arithmetic, by Francis Walkingame; published by Longmans in 1846.

Aunt Judy's Magazine: A Monthly Magazine For Young People, edited by Mrs. Alfred Gatty. Issues dated August 1867 and December 1870; published by Bell and Daldy.

The Monthly Packet, edited by Charlotte Yonge. Issue dated February 1880; published by Walter Smith.

Nature: A Weekly Illustrated Journal of Science. Issues dated 31 March 1887 and 14 October 1897; published by Macmillan.

The Life and Letters of Lewis Carroll, by Stuart Dodgson Collingwood; published by T. Fisher Unwin in 1898.

The Lewis Carroll Picture Book, by Stuart Dodgson Collingwood; published by T. Fisher Unwin in 1899.

Amusements in Mathematics, by Henry Dudeney; published by Nelson in 1917; reprinted by Dover in 1958.

The Collected Verse of Lewis Carroll; published by Macmillan in 1932.

Alice in Numberland, by Donald Eperson; privately printed in 1957.

The Magic of Lewis Carroll, edited by John Fisher; published by Nelson in 1973.

The Lewis Carroll Handbook, revised edition by Denis Crutch; published by Dawson Archon in 1979.

The Letters of Lewis Carroll, edited by Morton N. Cohen with the assistance of Roger Lancelyn Green; published by Macmillan in 1979.

Interviews and Recollections, edited by Morton N. Cohen; published by Macmillan in 1989.

The Cipher Alice, adapted and coded by Edward Wakeling; published by The Lewis Carroll Society Publications Unit in 1990.

Selections from the private papers of Professor Bartholomew Price, now in the Lewis Carroll Collection of Edward Wakeling.

THE WORKS OF LEWIS CARROLL

Alice's Adventures in Wonderland (1865)

Through the Looking-Glass (1871)

Doublets (1879)

Rhyme? and Reason? (1883)

A Tangled Tale (1885)

"Memoria Technica" (1888)

Sylvie and Bruno (1889)

"Syzygies and Lanrick" (1893)

A CATALOG OF SELECTED
DOVER BOOKS
IN ALL FIELDS OF INTEREST

A CATALOG OF SELECTED DOVER
BOOKS IN ALL FIELDS OF INTEREST

CONCERNING THE SPIRITUAL IN ART, Wassily Kandinsky. Pioneering work by father of abstract art. Thoughts on color theory, nature of art. Analysis of earlier masters. 12 illustrations. 80pp. of text. 5⅜ x 8½. 23411-8 Pa. $3.95

ANIMALS: 1,419 Copyright-Free Illustrations of Mammals, Birds, Fish, Insects, etc., Jim Harter (ed.). Clear wood engravings present, in extremely lifelike poses, over 1,000 species of animals. One of the most extensive pictorial sourcebooks of its kind. Captions. Index. 284pp. 9 x 12. 23766-4 Pa. $12.95

CELTIC ART: The Methods of Construction, George Bain. Simple geometric techniques for making Celtic interlacements, spirals, Kells-type initials, animals, humans, etc. Over 500 illustrations. 160pp. 9 x 12. (USO) 22923-8 Pa. $9.95

AN ATLAS OF ANATOMY FOR ARTISTS, Fritz Schider. Most thorough reference work on art anatomy in the world. Hundreds of illustrations, including selections from works by Vesalius, Leonardo, Goya, Ingres, Michelangelo, others. 593 illustrations. 192pp. 7⅛ x 10¼. 20241-0 Pa. $9.95

CELTIC HAND STROKE-BY-STROKE (Irish Half-Uncial from "The Book of Kells"): An Arthur Baker Calligraphy Manual, Arthur Baker. Complete guide to creating each letter of the alphabet in distinctive Celtic manner. Covers hand position, strokes, pens, inks, paper, more. Illustrated. 48pp. 8¼ x 11. 24336-2 Pa. $3.95

EASY ORIGAMI, John Montroll. Charming collection of 32 projects (hat, cup, pelican, piano, swan, many more) specially designed for the novice origami hobbyist. Clearly illustrated easy-to-follow instructions insure that even beginning papercrafters will achieve successful results. 48pp. 8¼ x 11. 27298-2 Pa. $3.50

THE COMPLETE BOOK OF BIRDHOUSE CONSTRUCTION FOR WOODWORKERS, Scott D. Campbell. Detailed instructions, illustrations, tables. Also data on bird habitat and instinct patterns. Bibliography. 3 tables. 63 illustrations in 15 figures. 48pp. 5¼ x 8½. 24407-5 Pa. $2.50

BLOOMINGDALE'S ILLUSTRATED 1886 CATALOG: Fashions, Dry Goods and Housewares, Bloomingdale Brothers. Famed merchants' extremely rare catalog depicting about 1,700 products: clothing, housewares, firearms, dry goods, jewelry, more. Invaluable for dating, identifying vintage items. Also, copyright-free graphics for artists, designers. Co-published with Henry Ford Museum & Greenfield Village. 160pp. 8¼ x 11. 25780-0 Pa. $10.95

HISTORIC COSTUME IN PICTURES, Braun & Schneider. Over 1,450 costumed figures in clearly detailed engravings–from dawn of civilization to end of 19th century. Captions. Many folk costumes. 256pp. 8⅜ x 11¾. 23150-X Pa. $12.95

STICKLEY CRAFTSMAN FURNITURE CATALOGS, Gustav Stickley and L. & J. G. Stickley. Beautiful, functional furniture in two authentic catalogs from 1910. 594 illustrations, including 277 photos, show settles, rockers, armchairs, reclining chairs, bookcases, desks, tables. 183pp. 6½ x 9¼. 23838-5 Pa. $9.95

AMERICAN LOCOMOTIVES IN HISTORIC PHOTOGRAPHS: 1858 to 1949, Ron Ziel (ed.). A rare collection of 126 meticulously detailed official photographs, called "builder portraits," of American locomotives that majestically chronicle the rise of steam locomotive power in America. Introduction. Detailed captions. xi + 129pp. 9 x 12. 27393-8 Pa. $12.95

AMERICA'S LIGHTHOUSES: An Illustrated History, Francis Ross Holland, Jr. Delightfully written, profusely illustrated fact-filled survey of over 200 American lighthouses since 1716. History, anecdotes, technological advances, more. 240pp. 8 x 10¾. 25576-X Pa. $12.95

TOWARDS A NEW ARCHITECTURE, Le Corbusier. Pioneering manifesto by founder of "International School." Technical and aesthetic theories, views of industry, economics, relation of form to function, "mass-production split" and much more. Profusely illustrated. 320pp. 6⅛ x 9¼. (USO) 25023-7 Pa. $9.95

HOW THE OTHER HALF LIVES, Jacob Riis. Famous journalistic record, exposing poverty and degradation of New York slums around 1900, by major social reformer. 100 striking and influential photographs. 233pp. 10 x 7⅞. 22012-5 Pa. $10.95

FRUIT KEY AND TWIG KEY TO TREES AND SHRUBS, William M. Harlow. One of the handiest and most widely used identification aids. Fruit key covers 120 deciduous and evergreen species; twig key 160 deciduous species. Easily used. Over 300 photographs. 126pp. 5⅜ x 8½. 20511-8 Pa. $3.95

COMMON BIRD SONGS, Dr. Donald J. Borror. Songs of 60 most common U.S. birds: robins, sparrows, cardinals, bluejays, finches, more—arranged in order of increasing complexity. Up to 9 variations of songs of each species. Cassette and manual 99911-4 $8.95

ORCHIDS AS HOUSE PLANTS, Rebecca Tyson Northen. Grow cattleyas and many other kinds of orchids—in a window, in a case, or under artificial light. 63 illustrations. 148pp. 5⅜ x 8½. 23261-1 Pa. $4.95

MONSTER MAZES, Dave Phillips. Masterful mazes at four levels of difficulty. Avoid deadly perils and evil creatures to find magical treasures. Solutions for all 32 exciting illustrated puzzles. 48pp. 8¼ x 11. 26005-4 Pa. $2.95

MOZART'S DON GIOVANNI (DOVER OPERA LIBRETTO SERIES), Wolfgang Amadeus Mozart. Introduced and translated by Ellen H. Bleiler. Standard Italian libretto, with complete English translation. Convenient and thoroughly portable—an ideal companion for reading along with a recording or the performance itself. Introduction. List of characters. Plot summary. 121pp. 5¼ x 8½. 24944-1 Pa. $2.95

TECHNICAL MANUAL AND DICTIONARY OF CLASSICAL BALLET, Gail Grant. Defines, explains, comments on steps, movements, poses and concepts. 15-page pictorial section. Basic book for student, viewer. 127pp. 5⅜ x 8½. 21843-0 Pa. $4.95

BRASS INSTRUMENTS: Their History and Development, Anthony Baines. Authoritative, updated survey of the evolution of trumpets, trombones, bugles, cornets, French horns, tubas and other brass wind instruments. Over 140 illustrations and 48 music examples. Corrected and updated by author. New preface. Bibliography. 320pp. 5⅜ x 8½. 27574-4 Pa. $9.95

HOLLYWOOD GLAMOR PORTRAITS, John Kobal (ed.). 145 photos from 1926-49. Harlow, Gable, Bogart, Bacall; 94 stars in all. Full background on photographers, technical aspects. 160pp. 8⅜ x 11¼. 23352-9 Pa. $12.95

MAX AND MORITZ, Wilhelm Busch. Great humor classic in both German and English. Also 10 other works: "Cat and Mouse," "Plisch and Plumm," etc. 216pp. 5⅜ x 8½. 20181-3 Pa. $6.95

THE RAVEN AND OTHER FAVORITE POEMS, Edgar Allan Poe. Over 40 of the author's most memorable poems: "The Bells," "Ulalume," "Israfel," "To Helen," "The Conqueror Worm," "Eldorado," "Annabel Lee," many more. Alphabetic lists of titles and first lines. 64pp. 5³⁄₁₆ x 8¼. 26685-0 Pa. $1.00

PERSONAL MEMOIRS OF U. S. GRANT, Ulysses Simpson Grant. Intelligent, deeply moving firsthand account of Civil War campaigns, considered by many the finest military memoirs ever written. Includes letters, historic photographs, maps and more. 528pp. 6⅛ x 9¼. 28587-1 Pa. $11.95

AMULETS AND SUPERSTITIONS, E. A. Wallis Budge. Comprehensive discourse on origin, powers of amulets in many ancient cultures: Arab, Persian Babylonian, Assyrian, Egyptian, Gnostic, Hebrew, Phoenician, Syriac, etc. Covers cross, swastika, crucifix, seals, rings, stones, etc. 584pp. 5⅜ x 8½. 23573-4 Pa. $12.95

RUSSIAN STORIES/PYCCKNE PACCKA3bl: A Dual-Language Book, edited by Gleb Struve. Twelve tales by such masters as Chekhov, Tolstoy, Dostoevsky, Pushkin, others. Excellent word-for-word English translations on facing pages, plus teaching and study aids, Russian/English vocabulary, biographical/critical introductions, more. 416pp. 5⅜ x 8½. 26244-8 Pa. $8.95

PHILADELPHIA THEN AND NOW: 60 Sites Photographed in the Past and Present, Kenneth Finkel and Susan Oyama. Rare photographs of City Hall, Logan Square, Independence Hall, Betsy Ross House, other landmarks juxtaposed with contemporary views. Captures changing face of historic city. Introduction. Captions. 128pp. 8¼ x 11. 25790-8 Pa. $9.95

AIA ARCHITECTURAL GUIDE TO NASSAU AND SUFFOLK COUNTIES, LONG ISLAND, The American Institute of Architects, Long Island Chapter, and the Society for the Preservation of Long Island Antiquities. Comprehensive, well-researched and generously illustrated volume brings to life over three centuries of Long Island's great architectural heritage. More than 240 photographs with authoritative, extensively detailed captions. 176pp. 8¼ x 11. 26946-9 Pa. $14.95

NORTH AMERICAN INDIAN LIFE: Customs and Traditions of 23 Tribes, Elsie Clews Parsons (ed.). 27 fictionalized essays by noted anthropologists examine religion, customs, government, additional facets of life among the Winnebago, Crow, Zuni, Eskimo, other tribes. 480pp. 6⅛ x 9¼. 27377-6 Pa. $10.95

FRANK LLOYD WRIGHT'S HOLLYHOCK HOUSE, Donald Hoffmann. Lavishly illustrated, carefully documented study of one of Wright's most controversial residential designs. Over 120 photographs, floor plans, elevations, etc. Detailed perceptive text by noted Wright scholar. Index. 128pp. 9¼ x 10¾. 27133-1 Pa. $11.95

THE MALE AND FEMALE FIGURE IN MOTION: 60 Classic Photographic Sequences, Eadweard Muybridge. 60 true-action photographs of men and women walking, running, climbing, bending, turning, etc., reproduced from rare 19th-century masterpiece. vi + 121pp. 9 x 12. 24745-7 Pa. $10.95

1001 QUESTIONS ANSWERED ABOUT THE SEASHORE, N. J. Berrill and Jacquelyn Berrill. Queries answered about dolphins, sea snails, sponges, starfish, fishes, shore birds, many others. Covers appearance, breeding, growth, feeding, much more. 305pp. 5¼ x 8¼. 23366-9 Pa. $8.95

GUIDE TO OWL WATCHING IN NORTH AMERICA, Donald S. Heintzelman. Superb guide offers complete data and descriptions of 19 species: barn owl, screech owl, snowy owl, many more. Expert coverage of owl-watching equipment, conservation, migrations and invasions, etc. Guide to observing sites. 84 illustrations. xiii + 193pp. 5⅜ x 8½. 27344-X Pa. $8.95

MEDICINAL AND OTHER USES OF NORTH AMERICAN PLANTS: A Historical Survey with Special Reference to the Eastern Indian Tribes, Charlotte Erichsen-Brown. Chronological historical citations document 500 years of usage of plants, trees, shrubs native to eastern Canada, northeastern U.S. Also complete identifying information. 343 illustrations. 544pp. 6½ x 9¼. 25951-X Pa. $12.95

STORYBOOK MAZES, Dave Phillips. 23 stories and mazes on two-page spreads: Wizard of Oz, Treasure Island, Robin Hood, etc. Solutions. 64pp. 8¼ x 11. 23628-5 Pa. $2.95

NEGRO FOLK MUSIC, U.S.A., Harold Courlander. Noted folklorist's scholarly yet readable analysis of rich and varied musical tradition. Includes authentic versions of over 40 folk songs. Valuable bibliography and discography. xi + 324pp. 5⅜ x 8½. 27350-4 Pa. $9.95

MOVIE-STAR PORTRAITS OF THE FORTIES, John Kobal (ed.). 163 glamor, studio photos of 106 stars of the 1940s: Rita Hayworth, Ava Gardner, Marlon Brando, Clark Gable, many more. 176pp. 8⅜ x 11¼. 23546-7 Pa. $12.95

BENCHLEY LOST AND FOUND, Robert Benchley. Finest humor from early 30s, about pet peeves, child psychologists, post office and others. Mostly unavailable elsewhere. 73 illustrations by Peter Arno and others. 183pp. 5⅜ x 8½. 22410-4 Pa. $6.95

YEKL and THE IMPORTED BRIDEGROOM AND OTHER STORIES OF YIDDISH NEW YORK, Abraham Cahan. Film Hester Street based on Yekl (1896). Novel, other stories among first about Jewish immigrants on N.Y.'s East Side. 240pp. 5⅜ x 8½. 22427-9 Pa. $6.95

SELECTED POEMS, Walt Whitman. Generous sampling from *Leaves of Grass.* Twenty-four poems include "I Hear America Singing," "Song of the Open Road," "I Sing the Body Electric," "When Lilacs Last in the Dooryard Bloom'd," "O Captain! My Captain!"–all reprinted from an authoritative edition. Lists of titles and first lines. 128pp. 5³⁄₁₆ x 8¼. 26878-0 Pa. $1.00

THE BEST TALES OF HOFFMANN, E. T. A. Hoffmann. 10 of Hoffmann's most important stories: "Nutcracker and the King of Mice," "The Golden Flowerpot," etc. 458pp. 5⅜ x 8½. 21793-0 Pa. $9.95

FROM FETISH TO GOD IN ANCIENT EGYPT, E. A. Wallis Budge. Rich detailed survey of Egyptian conception of "God" and gods, magic, cult of animals, Osiris, more. Also, superb English translations of hymns and legends. 240 illustrations. 545pp. 5⅜ x 8½. 25803-3 Pa. $13.95

FRENCH STORIES/CONTES FRANÇAIS: A Dual-Language Book, Wallace Fowlie. Ten stories by French masters, Voltaire to Camus: "Micromegas" by Voltaire; "The Atheist's Mass" by Balzac; "Minuet" by de Maupassant; "The Guest" by Camus, six more. Excellent English translations on facing pages. Also French-English vocabulary list, exercises, more. 352pp. 5⅜ x 8½. 26443-2 Pa. $8.95

CHICAGO AT THE TURN OF THE CENTURY IN PHOTOGRAPHS: 122 Historic Views from the Collections of the Chicago Historical Society, Larry A. Viskochil. Rare large-format prints offer detailed views of City Hall, State Street, the Loop, Hull House, Union Station, many other landmarks, circa 1904-1913. Introduction. Captions. Maps. 144pp. 9⅜ x 12¼. 24656-6 Pa. $12.95

OLD BROOKLYN IN EARLY PHOTOGRAPHS, 1865-1929, William Lee Younger. Luna Park, Gravesend race track, construction of Grand Army Plaza, moving of Hotel Brighton, etc. 157 previously unpublished photographs. 165pp. 8⅞ x 11¾. 23587-4 Pa. $13.95

THE MYTHS OF THE NORTH AMERICAN INDIANS, Lewis Spence. Rich anthology of the myths and legends of the Algonquins, Iroquois, Pawnees and Sioux, prefaced by an extensive historical and ethnological commentary. 36 illustrations. 480pp. 5⅜ x 8½. 25967-6 Pa. $8.95

AN ENCYCLOPEDIA OF BATTLES: Accounts of Over 1,560 Battles from 1479 B.C. to the Present, David Eggenberger. Essential details of every major battle in recorded history from the first battle of Megiddo in 1479 B.C. to Grenada in 1984. List of Battle Maps. New Appendix covering the years 1967-1984. Index. 99 illustrations. 544pp. 6½ x 9¼. 24913-1 Pa. $14.95

SAILING ALONE AROUND THE WORLD, Captain Joshua Slocum. First man to sail around the world, alone, in small boat. One of great feats of seamanship told in delightful manner. 67 illustrations. 294pp. 5⅜ x 8½. 20326-3 Pa. $5.95

ANARCHISM AND OTHER ESSAYS, Emma Goldman. Powerful, penetrating, prophetic essays on direct action, role of minorities, prison reform, puritan hypocrisy, violence, etc. 271pp. 5⅜ x 8½. 22484-8 Pa. $6.95

MYTHS OF THE HINDUS AND BUDDHISTS, Ananda K. Coomaraswamy and Sister Nivedita. Great stories of the epics; deeds of Krishna, Shiva, taken from puranas, Vedas, folk tales; etc. 32 illustrations. 400pp. 5⅜ x 8½. 21759-0 Pa. $10.95

BEYOND PSYCHOLOGY, Otto Rank. Fear of death, desire of immortality, nature of sexuality, social organization, creativity, according to Rankian system. 291pp. 5⅜ x 8½. 20485-5 Pa. $8.95

A THEOLOGICO-POLITICAL TREATISE, Benedict Spinoza. Also contains unfinished Political Treatise. Great classic on religious liberty, theory of government on common consent. R. Elwes translation. Total of 421pp. 5⅜ x 8½. 20249-6 Pa. $9.95

MY BONDAGE AND MY FREEDOM, Frederick Douglass. Born a slave, Douglass became outspoken force in antislavery movement. The best of Douglass' autobiographies. Graphic description of slave life. 464pp. 5⅜ x 8½. 22457-0 Pa. $8.95

FOLLOWING THE EQUATOR: A Journey Around the World, Mark Twain. Fascinating humorous account of 1897 voyage to Hawaii, Australia, India, New Zealand, etc. Ironic, bemused reports on peoples, customs, climate, flora and fauna, politics, much more. 197 illustrations. 720pp. 5⅜ x 8½. 26113-1 Pa. $15.95

THE PEOPLE CALLED SHAKERS, Edward D. Andrews. Definitive study of Shakers: origins, beliefs, practices, dances, social organization, furniture and crafts, etc. 33 illustrations. 351pp. 5⅜ x 8½. 21081-2 Pa. $8.95

THE MYTHS OF GREECE AND ROME, H. A. Guerber. A classic of mythology, generously illustrated, long prized for its simple, graphic, accurate retelling of the principal myths of Greece and Rome, and for its commentary on their origins and significance. With 64 illustrations by Michelangelo, Raphael, Titian, Rubens, Canova, Bernini and others. 480pp. 5⅜ x 8½. 27584-1 Pa. $9.95

PSYCHOLOGY OF MUSIC, Carl E. Seashore. Classic work discusses music as a medium from psychological viewpoint. Clear treatment of physical acoustics, auditory apparatus, sound perception, development of musical skills, nature of musical feeling, host of other topics. 88 figures. 408pp. 5⅜ x 8½. 21851-1 Pa. $10.95

THE PHILOSOPHY OF HISTORY, Georg W. Hegel. Great classic of Western thought develops concept that history is not chance but rational process, the evolution of freedom. 457pp. 5⅜ x 8½. 20112-0 Pa. $9.95

THE BOOK OF TEA, Kakuzo Okakura. Minor classic of the Orient: entertaining, charming explanation, interpretation of traditional Japanese culture in terms of tea ceremony. 94pp. 5⅜ x 8½. 20070-1 Pa. $3.95

LIFE IN ANCIENT EGYPT, Adolf Erman. Fullest, most thorough, detailed older account with much not in more recent books, domestic life, religion, magic, medicine, commerce, much more. Many illustrations reproduce tomb paintings, carvings, hieroglyphs, etc. 597pp. 5⅜ x 8½. 22632-8 Pa. $11.95

SUNDIALS, Their Theory and Construction, Albert Waugh. Far and away the best, most thorough coverage of ideas, mathematics concerned, types, construction, adjusting anywhere. Simple, nontechnical treatment allows even children to build several of these dials. Over 100 illustrations. 230pp. 5⅜ x 8½. 22947-5 Pa. $7.95

DYNAMICS OF FLUIDS IN POROUS MEDIA, Jacob Bear. For advanced students of ground water hydrology, soil mechanics and physics, drainage and irrigation engineering, and more. 335 illustrations. Exercises, with answers. 784pp. 6⅛ x 9¼.
65675-6 Pa. $19.95

SONGS OF EXPERIENCE: Facsimile Reproduction with 26 Plates in Full Color, William Blake. 26 full-color plates from a rare 1826 edition. Includes "TheTyger," "London," "Holy Thursday," and other poems. Printed text of poems. 48pp. 5¼ x 7.
24636-1 Pa. $4.95

OLD-TIME VIGNETTES IN FULL COLOR, Carol Belanger Grafton (ed.). Over 390 charming, often sentimental illustrations, selected from archives of Victorian graphics—pretty women posing, children playing, food, flowers, kittens and puppies, smiling cherubs, birds and butterflies, much more. All copyright-free. 48pp. 9¼ x 12¼.
27269-9 Pa. $7.95

PERSPECTIVE FOR ARTISTS, Rex Vicat Cole. Depth, perspective of sky and sea, shadows, much more, not usually covered. 391 diagrams, 81 reproductions of drawings and paintings. 279pp. 5⅜ x 8½. 22487-2 Pa. $7.95

DRAWING THE LIVING FIGURE, Joseph Sheppard. Innovative approach to artistic anatomy focuses on specifics of surface anatomy, rather than muscles and bones. Over 170 drawings of live models in front, back and side views, and in widely varying poses. Accompanying diagrams. 177 illustrations. Introduction. Index. 144pp. 8⅜ x11¼. 26723-7 Pa. $8.95

GOTHIC AND OLD ENGLISH ALPHABETS: 100 Complete Fonts, Dan X. Solo. Add power, elegance to posters, signs, other graphics with 100 stunning copyright-free alphabets: Blackstone, Dolbey, Germania, 97 more–including many lower-case, numerals, punctuation marks. 104pp. 8⅛ x 11. 24695-7 Pa. $8.95

HOW TO DO BEADWORK, Mary White. Fundamental book on craft from simple projects to five-bead chains and woven works. 106 illustrations. 142pp. 5⅜ x 8. 20697-1 Pa. $4.95

THE BOOK OF WOOD CARVING, Charles Marshall Sayers. Finest book for beginners discusses fundamentals and offers 34 designs. "Absolutely first rate . . . well thought out and well executed."–E. J. Tangerman. 118pp. 7¾ x 10⅝. 23654-4 Pa. $6.95

ILLUSTRATED CATALOG OF CIVIL WAR MILITARY GOODS: Union Army Weapons, Insignia, Uniform Accessories, and Other Equipment, Schuyler, Hartley, and Graham. Rare, profusely illustrated 1846 catalog includes Union Army uniform and dress regulations, arms and ammunition, coats, insignia, flags, swords, rifles, etc. 226 illustrations. 160pp. 9 x 12. 24939-5 Pa. $10.95

WOMEN'S FASHIONS OF THE EARLY 1900s: An Unabridged Republication of "New York Fashions, 1909," National Cloak & Suit Co. Rare catalog of mail-order fashions documents women's and children's clothing styles shortly after the turn of the century. Captions offer full descriptions, prices. Invaluable resource for fashion, costume historians. Approximately 725 illustrations. 128pp. 8⅜ x 11¼. 27276-1 Pa. $11.95

THE 1912 AND 1915 GUSTAV STICKLEY FURNITURE CATALOGS, Gustav Stickley. With over 200 detailed illustrations and descriptions, these two catalogs are essential reading and reference materials and identification guides for Stickley furniture. Captions cite materials, dimensions and prices. 112pp. 6½ x 9¼. 26676-1 Pa. $9.95

EARLY AMERICAN LOCOMOTIVES, John H. White, Jr. Finest locomotive engravings from early 19th century: historical (1804–74), main-line (after 1870), special, foreign, etc. 147 plates. 142pp. 11⅜ x 8¼. 22772-3 Pa. $10.95

THE TALL SHIPS OF TODAY IN PHOTOGRAPHS, Frank O. Braynard. Lavishly illustrated tribute to nearly 100 majestic contemporary sailing vessels: Amerigo Vespucci, Clearwater, Constitution, Eagle, Mayflower, Sea Cloud, Victory, many more. Authoritative captions provide statistics, background on each ship. 190 black-and-white photographs and illustrations. Introduction. 128pp. 8⅞ x 11¾. 27163-3 Pa. $13.95

EARLY NINETEENTH-CENTURY CRAFTS AND TRADES, Peter Stockham (ed.). Extremely rare 1807 volume describes to youngsters the crafts and trades of the day: brickmaker, weaver, dressmaker, bookbinder, ropemaker, saddler, many more. Quaint prose, charming illustrations for each craft. 20 black-and-white line illustrations. 192pp. 4⅝ x 6. 27293-1 Pa. $4.95

VICTORIAN FASHIONS AND COSTUMES FROM HARPER'S BAZAR, 1867–1898, Stella Blum (ed.). Day costumes, evening wear, sports clothes, shoes, hats, other accessories in over 1,000 detailed engravings. 320pp. 9⅜ x 12¼. 22990-4 Pa. $14.95

GUSTAV STICKLEY, THE CRAFTSMAN, Mary Ann Smith. Superb study surveys broad scope of Stickley's achievement, especially in architecture. Design philosophy, rise and fall of the Craftsman empire, descriptions and floor plans for many Craftsman houses, more. 86 black-and-white halftones. 31 line illustrations. Introduction 208pp. 6½ x 9¼. 27210-9 Pa. $9.95

THE LONG ISLAND RAIL ROAD IN EARLY PHOTOGRAPHS, Ron Ziel. Over 220 rare photos, informative text document origin (1844) and development of rail service on Long Island. Vintage views of early trains, locomotives, stations, passengers, crews, much more. Captions. 8⅞ x 11¾. 26301-0 Pa. $13.95

THE BOOK OF OLD SHIPS: From Egyptian Galleys to Clipper Ships, Henry B. Culver. Superb, authoritative history of sailing vessels, with 80 magnificent line illustrations. Galley, bark, caravel, longship, whaler, many more. Detailed, informative text on each vessel by noted naval historian. Introduction. 256pp. 5⅜ x 8½. 27332-6 Pa. $7.95

TEN BOOKS ON ARCHITECTURE, Vitruvius. The most important book ever written on architecture. Early Roman aesthetics, technology, classical orders, site selection, all other aspects. Morgan translation. 331pp. 5⅜ x 8½. 20645-9 Pa. $8.95

THE HUMAN FIGURE IN MOTION, Eadweard Muybridge. More than 4,500 stopped-action photos, in action series, showing undraped men, women, children jumping, lying down, throwing, sitting, wrestling, carrying, etc. 390pp. 7⅞ x 10⅝. 20204-6 Clothbd. $25.95

TREES OF THE EASTERN AND CENTRAL UNITED STATES AND CANADA, William M. Harlow. Best one-volume guide to 140 trees. Full descriptions, woodlore, range, etc. Over 600 illustrations. Handy size. 288pp. 4½ x 6⅜. 20395-6 Pa. $6.95

SONGS OF WESTERN BIRDS, Dr. Donald J. Borror. Complete song and call repertoire of 60 western species, including flycatchers, juncoes, cactus wrens, many more–includes fully illustrated booklet. Cassette and manual 99913-0 $8.95

GROWING AND USING HERBS AND SPICES, Milo Miloradovich. Versatile handbook provides all the information needed for cultivation and use of all the herbs and spices available in North America. 4 illustrations. Index. Glossary. 236pp. 5⅜ x 8½. 25058-X Pa. $6.95

BIG BOOK OF MAZES AND LABYRINTHS, Walter Shepherd. 50 mazes and labyrinths in all–classical, solid, ripple, and more–in one great volume. Perfect inexpensive puzzler for clever youngsters. Full solutions. 112pp. 8⅛ x 11. 22951-3 Pa. $4.95

PIANO TUNING, J. Cree Fischer. Clearest, best book for beginner, amateur. Simple repairs, raising dropped notes, tuning by easy method of flattened fifths. No previous skills needed. 4 illustrations. 201pp. 5⅜ x 8½. 23267-0 Pa. $6.95

A SOURCE BOOK IN THEATRICAL HISTORY, A. M. Nagler. Contemporary observers on acting, directing, make-up, costuming, stage props, machinery, scene design, from Ancient Greece to Chekhov. 611pp. 5⅜ x 8½. 20515-0 Pa. $12.95

THE COMPLETE NONSENSE OF EDWARD LEAR, Edward Lear. All nonsense limericks, zany alphabets, Owl and Pussycat, songs, nonsense botany, etc., illustrated by Lear. Total of 320pp. 5⅜ x 8½. (USO) 20167-8 Pa. $6.95

VICTORIAN PARLOUR POETRY: An Annotated Anthology, Michael R. Turner. 117 gems by Longfellow, Tennyson, Browning, many lesser-known poets. "The Village Blacksmith," "Curfew Must Not Ring Tonight," "Only a Baby Small," dozens more, often difficult to find elsewhere. Index of poets, titles, first lines. xxiii + 325pp. 5⅝ x 8¼. 27044-0 Pa. $8.95

DUBLINERS, James Joyce. Fifteen stories offer vivid, tightly focused observations of the lives of Dublin's poorer classes. At least one, "The Dead," is considered a masterpiece. Reprinted complete and unabridged from standard edition. 160pp. 5³⁄₁₆ x 8¼. 26870-5 Pa. $1.00

THE HAUNTED MONASTERY and THE CHINESE MAZE MURDERS, Robert van Gulik. Two full novels by van Gulik, set in 7th-century China, continue adventures of Judge Dee and his companions. An evil Taoist monastery, seemingly supernatural events; overgrown topiary maze hides strange crimes. 27 illustrations. 328pp. 5⅜ x 8½. 23502-5 Pa. $8.95

THE BOOK OF THE SACRED MAGIC OF ABRAMELIN THE MAGE, translated by S. MacGregor Mathers. Medieval manuscript of ceremonial magic. Basic document in Aleister Crowley, Golden Dawn groups. 268pp. 5⅜ x 8½. 23211-5 Pa. $8.95

NEW RUSSIAN-ENGLISH AND ENGLISH-RUSSIAN DICTIONARY, M. A. O'Brien. This is a remarkably handy Russian dictionary, containing a surprising amount of information, including over 70,000 entries. 366pp. 4½ x 6⅛. 20208-9 Pa. $9.95

HISTORIC HOMES OF THE AMERICAN PRESIDENTS, Second, Revised Edition, Irvin Haas. A traveler's guide to American Presidential homes, most open to the public, depicting and describing homes occupied by every American President from George Washington to George Bush. With visiting hours, admission charges, travel routes. 175 photographs. Index. 160pp. 8¼ x 11. 26751-2 Pa. $11.95

NEW YORK IN THE FORTIES, Andreas Feininger. 162 brilliant photographs by the well-known photographer, formerly with *Life* magazine. Commuters, shoppers, Times Square at night, much else from city at its peak. Captions by John von Hartz. 181pp. 9¼ x 10¾. 23585-8 Pa. $12.95

INDIAN SIGN LANGUAGE, William Tomkins. Over 525 signs developed by Sioux and other tribes. Written instructions and diagrams. Also 290 pictographs. 111pp. 6⅛ x 9¼. 22029-X Pa. $3.95

CATALOG OF DOVER BOOKS

ANATOMY: A Complete Guide for Artists, Joseph Sheppard. A master of figure drawing shows artists how to render human anatomy convincingly. Over 460 illustrations. 224pp. 8⅜ x 11¼. 27279-6 Pa. $10.95

MEDIEVAL CALLIGRAPHY: Its History and Technique, Marc Drogin. Spirited history, comprehensive instruction manual covers 13 styles (ca. 4th century thru 15th). Excellent photographs; directions for duplicating medieval techniques with modern tools. 224pp. 8⅜ x 11¼. 26142-5 Pa. $12.95

DRIED FLOWERS: How to Prepare Them, Sarah Whitlock and Martha Rankin. Complete instructions on how to use silica gel, meal and borax, perlite aggregate, sand and borax, glycerine and water to create attractive permanent flower arrangements. 12 illustrations. 32pp. 5⅜ x 8½. 21802-3 Pa. $1.00

EASY TO MAKE BIRD FEEDERS FOR WOODWORKERS, Scott D. Campbell. Detailed, simple-to-use guide for designing, constructing, caring for and using feeders. Text, illustrations for 12 classic and contemporary designs. 96pp. 5⅜ x 8½. 25847-5 Pa. $2.95

SCOTTISH WONDER TALES FROM MYTH AND LEGEND, Donald A. Mackenzie. 16 lively tales tell of giants rumbling down mountainsides, of a magic wand that turns stone pillars into warriors, of gods and goddesses, evil hags, powerful forces and more. 240pp. 5⅜ x 8½. 29677-6 Pa. $6.95

THE HISTORY OF UNDERCLOTHES, C. Willett Cunnington and Phyllis Cunnington. Fascinating, well-documented survey covering six centuries of English undergarments, enhanced with over 100 illustrations: 12th-century laced-up bodice, footed long drawers (1795), 19th-century bustles, 19th-century corsets for men, Victorian "bust improvers," much more. 272pp. 5⅜ x 8¼. 27124-2 Pa. $9.95

ARTS AND CRAFTS FURNITURE: The Complete Brooks Catalog of 1912, Brooks Manufacturing Co. Photos and detailed descriptions of more than 150 now very collectible furniture designs from the Arts and Crafts movement depict davenports, settees, buffets, desks, tables, chairs, bedsteads, dressers and more, all built of solid, quarter-sawed oak. Invaluable for students and enthusiasts of antiques, Americana and the decorative arts. 80pp. 6½ x 9¼. 27471-3 Pa. $8.95

HOW WE INVENTED THE AIRPLANE: An Illustrated History, Orville Wright. Fascinating firsthand account covers early experiments, construction of planes and motors, first flights, much more. Introduction and commentary by Fred C. Kelly. 76 photographs. 96pp. 8¼ x 11. 25662-6 Pa. $8.95

THE ARTS OF THE SAILOR: Knotting, Splicing and Ropework, Hervey Garrett Smith. Indispensable shipboard reference covers tools, basic knots and useful hitches; handsewing and canvas work, more. Over 100 illustrations. Delightful reading for sea lovers. 256pp. 5⅜ x 8½. 26440-8 Pa. $7.95

FRANK LLOYD WRIGHT'S FALLINGWATER: The House and Its History, Second, Revised Edition, Donald Hoffmann. A total revision—both in text and illustrations—of the standard document on Fallingwater, the boldest, most personal architectural statement of Wright's mature years, updated with valuable new material from the recently opened Frank Lloyd Wright Archives. "Fascinating"–*The New York Times*. 116 illustrations. 128pp. 9¼ x 10¾. 27430-6 Pa. $11.95

PHOTOGRAPHIC SKETCHBOOK OF THE CIVIL WAR, Alexander Gardner. 100 photos taken on field during the Civil War. Famous shots of Manassas Harper's Ferry, Lincoln, Richmond, slave pens, etc. 244pp. 10⅝ x 8¼. 22731-6 Pa. $9.95

FIVE ACRES AND INDEPENDENCE, Maurice G. Kains. Great back-to-the-land classic explains basics of self-sufficient farming. The one book to get. 95 illustrations. 397pp. 5⅜ x 8½. 20974-1 Pa. $7.95

SONGS OF EASTERN BIRDS, Dr. Donald J. Borror. Songs and calls of 60 species most common to eastern U.S.: warblers, woodpeckers, flycatchers, thrushes, larks, many more in high-quality recording. Cassette and manual 99912-2 $9.95

A MODERN HERBAL, Margaret Grieve. Much the fullest, most exact, most useful compilation of herbal material. Gigantic alphabetical encyclopedia, from aconite to zedoary, gives botanical information, medical properties, folklore, economic uses, much else. Indispensable to serious reader. 161 illustrations. 888pp. 6½ x 9¼. 2-vol. set. (USO)
Vol. I: 22798-7 Pa. $9.95
Vol. II: 22799-5 Pa. $9.95

HIDDEN TREASURE MAZE BOOK, Dave Phillips. Solve 34 challenging mazes accompanied by heroic tales of adventure. Evil dragons, people-eating plants, blood-thirsty giants, many more dangerous adversaries lurk at every twist and turn. 34 mazes, stories, solutions. 48pp. 8¼ x 11. 24566-7 Pa. $2.95

LETTERS OF W. A. MOZART, Wolfgang A. Mozart. Remarkable letters show bawdy wit, humor, imagination, musical insights, contemporary musical world; includes some letters from Leopold Mozart. 276pp. 5⅜ x 8½. 22859-2 Pa. $7.95

BASIC PRINCIPLES OF CLASSICAL BALLET, Agrippina Vaganova. Great Russian theoretician, teacher explains methods for teaching classical ballet. 118 illustrations. 175pp. 5⅜ x 8½. 22036-2 Pa. $5.95

THE JUMPING FROG, Mark Twain. Revenge edition. The original story of The Celebrated Jumping Frog of Calaveras County, a hapless French translation, and Twain's hilarious "retranslation" from the French. 12 illustrations. 66pp. 5⅜ x 8½. 22686-7 Pa. $3.95

BEST REMEMBERED POEMS, Martin Gardner (ed.). The 126 poems in this superb collection of 19th- and 20th-century British and American verse range from Shelley's "To a Skylark" to the impassioned "Renascence" of Edna St. Vincent Millay and to Edward Lear's whimsical "The Owl and the Pussycat." 224pp. 5⅜ x 8½. 27165-X Pa. $4.95

COMPLETE SONNETS, William Shakespeare. Over 150 exquisite poems deal with love, friendship, the tyranny of time, beauty's evanescence, death and other themes in language of remarkable power, precision and beauty. Glossary of archaic terms. 80pp. 5³⁄₁₆ x 8¼. 26686-9 Pa. $1.00

BODIES IN A BOOKSHOP, R. T. Campbell. Challenging mystery of blackmail and murder with ingenious plot and superbly drawn characters. In the best tradition of British suspense fiction. 192pp. 5⅜ x 8½. 24720-1 Pa. $6.95

CATALOG OF DOVER BOOKS

THE WIT AND HUMOR OF OSCAR WILDE, Alvin Redman (ed.). More than 1,000 ripostes, paradoxes, wisecracks: Work is the curse of the drinking classes; I can resist everything except temptation; etc. 258pp. 5⅜ x 8½. 20602-5 Pa. $5.95

SHAKESPEARE LEXICON AND QUOTATION DICTIONARY, Alexander Schmidt. Full definitions, locations, shades of meaning in every word in plays and poems. More than 50,000 exact quotations. 1,485pp. 6½ x 9¼. 2-vol. set.
Vol. 1: 22726-X Pa. $16.95
Vol. 2: 22727-8 Pa. $16.95

SELECTED POEMS, Emily Dickinson. Over 100 best-known, best-loved poems by one of America's foremost poets, reprinted from authoritative early editions. No comparable edition at this price. Index of first lines. 64pp. 5³⁄₁₆ x 8¼. 26466-1 Pa. $1.00

CELEBRATED CASES OF JUDGE DEE (DEE GOONG AN), translated by Robert van Gulik. Authentic 18th-century Chinese detective novel; Dee and associates solve three interlocked cases. Led to van Gulik's own stories with same characters. Extensive introduction. 9 illustrations. 237pp. 5⅜ x 8½. 23337-5 Pa. $6.95

THE MALLEUS MALEFICARUM OF KRAMER AND SPRENGER, translated by Montague Summers. Full text of most important witchhunter's "bible," used by both Catholics and Protestants. 278pp. 6⅝ x 10. 22802-9 Pa. $12.95

SPANISH STORIES/CUENTOS ESPAÑOLES: A Dual-Language Book, Angel Flores (ed.). Unique format offers 13 great stories in Spanish by Cervantes, Borges, others. Faithful English translations on facing pages. 352pp. 5⅜ x 8½. 25399-6 Pa. $8.95

THE CHICAGO WORLD'S FAIR OF 1893: A Photographic Record, Stanley Appelbaum (ed.). 128 rare photos show 200 buildings, Beaux-Arts architecture, Midway, original Ferris Wheel, Edison's kinetoscope, more. Architectural emphasis; full text. 116pp. 8¼ x 11. 23990-X Pa. $9.95

OLD QUEENS, N.Y., IN EARLY PHOTOGRAPHS, Vincent F. Seyfried and William Asadorian. Over 160 rare photographs of Maspeth, Jamaica, Jackson Heights, and other areas. Vintage views of DeWitt Clinton mansion, 1939 World's Fair and more. Captions. 192pp. 8⅞ x 11. 26358-4 Pa. $12.95

CAPTURED BY THE INDIANS: 15 Firsthand Accounts, 1750-1870, Frederick Drimmer. Astounding true historical accounts of grisly torture, bloody conflicts, relentless pursuits, miraculous escapes and more, by people who lived to tell the tale. 384pp. 5⅜ x 8½. 24901-8 Pa. $8.95

THE WORLD'S GREAT SPEECHES, Lewis Copeland and Lawrence W. Lamm (eds.). Vast collection of 278 speeches of Greeks to 1970. Powerful and effective models; unique look at history. 842pp. 5⅜ x 8½. 20468-5 Pa. $14.95

THE BOOK OF THE SWORD, Sir Richard F. Burton. Great Victorian scholar/adventurer's eloquent, erudite history of the "queen of weapons"—from prehistory to early Roman Empire. Evolution and development of early swords, variations (sabre, broadsword, cutlass, scimitar, etc.), much more. 336pp. 6⅛ x 9¼. 25434-8 Pa. $9.95

CATALOG OF DOVER BOOKS

AUTOBIOGRAPHY: The Story of My Experiments with Truth, Mohandas K. Gandhi. Boyhood, legal studies, purification, the growth of the Satyagraha (nonviolent protest) movement. Critical, inspiring work of the man responsible for the freedom of India. 480pp. 5⅜ x 8½. (USO)   24593-4 Pa. $8.95

CELTIC MYTHS AND LEGENDS, T. W. Rolleston. Masterful retelling of Irish and Welsh stories and tales. Cuchulain, King Arthur, Deirdre, the Grail, many more. First paperback edition. 58 full-page illustrations. 512pp. 5⅜ x 8½.   26507-2 Pa. $9.95

THE PRINCIPLES OF PSYCHOLOGY, William James. Famous long course complete, unabridged. Stream of thought, time perception, memory, experimental methods; great work decades ahead of its time. 94 figures. 1,391pp. 5⅜ x 8½. 2-vol. set.
Vol. I: 20381-6 Pa. $12.95
Vol. II: 20382-4 Pa. $12.95

THE WORLD AS WILL AND REPRESENTATION, Arthur Schopenhauer. Definitive English translation of Schopenhauer's life work, correcting more than 1,000 errors, omissions in earlier translations. Translated by E. F. J. Payne. Total of 1,269pp. 5⅜ x 8½. 2-vol. set.
Vol. 1: 21761-2 Pa. $11.95
Vol. 2: 21762-0 Pa. $12.95

MAGIC AND MYSTERY IN TIBET, Madame Alexandra David-Neel. Experiences among lamas, magicians, sages, sorcerers, Bonpa wizards. A true psychic discovery. 32 illustrations. 321pp. 5⅜ x 8½. (USO)   22682-4 Pa. $8.95

THE EGYPTIAN BOOK OF THE DEAD, E. A. Wallis Budge. Complete reproduction of Ani's papyrus, finest ever found. Full hieroglyphic text, interlinear transliteration, word-for-word translation, smooth translation. 533pp. 6½ x 9¼.
21866-X Pa. $10.95

MATHEMATICS FOR THE NONMATHEMATICIAN, Morris Kline. Detailed, college-level treatment of mathematics in cultural and historical context, with numerous exercises. Recommended Reading Lists. Tables. Numerous figures. 641pp. 5⅜ x 8½.
24823-2 Pa. $11.95

THEORY OF WING SECTIONS: Including a Summary of Airfoil Data, Ira H. Abbott and A. E. von Doenhoff. Concise compilation of subsonic aerodynamic characteristics of NACA wing sections, plus description of theory. 350pp. of tables. 693pp. 5⅜ x 8½.   60586-8 Pa. $14.95

THE RIME OF THE ANCIENT MARINER, Gustave Doré, S. T. Coleridge. Doré's finest work; 34 plates capture moods, subtleties of poem. Flawless full-size reproductions printed on facing pages with authoritative text of poem. "Beautiful. Simply beautiful."—*Publisher's Weekly.* 77pp. 9¼ x 12.   22305-1 Pa. $6.95

NORTH AMERICAN INDIAN DESIGNS FOR ARTISTS AND CRAFTSPEOPLE, Eva Wilson. Over 360 authentic copyright-free designs adapted from Navajo blankets, Hopi pottery, Sioux buffalo hides, more. Geometrics, symbolic figures, plant and animal motifs, etc. 128pp. 8⅜ x 11. (EUK)   25341-4 Pa. $8.95

SCULPTURE: Principles and Practice, Louis Slobodkin. Step-by-step approach to clay, plaster, metals, stone; classical and modern. 253 drawings, photos. 255pp. 8⅛ x 11.
22960-2 Pa. $11.95

THE INFLUENCE OF SEA POWER UPON HISTORY, 1660–1783, A. T. Mahan. Influential classic of naval history and tactics still used as text in war colleges. First paperback edition. 4 maps. 24 battle plans. 640pp. 5⅜ x 8½.   25509-3 Pa. $12.95

THE STORY OF THE TITANIC AS TOLD BY ITS SURVIVORS, Jack Winocour (ed.). What it was really like. Panic, despair, shocking inefficiency, and a little heroism. More thrilling than any fictional account. 26 illustrations. 320pp. 5⅜ x 8½.   20610-6 Pa. $8.95

FAIRY AND FOLK TALES OF THE IRISH PEASANTRY, William Butler Yeats (ed.). Treasury of 64 tales from the twilight world of Celtic myth and legend: "The Soul Cages," "The Kildare Pooka," "King O'Toole and his Goose," many more. Introduction and Notes by W. B. Yeats. 352pp. 5⅜ x 8½.   26941-8 Pa. $8.95

BUDDHIST MAHAYANA TEXTS, E. B. Cowell and Others (eds.). Superb, accurate translations of basic documents in Mahayana Buddhism, highly important in history of religions. The Buddha-karita of Asvaghosha, Larger Sukhavativyuha, more. 448pp. 5⅜ x 8½.   25552-2 Pa. $12.95

ONE TWO THREE . . . INFINITY: Facts and Speculations of Science, George Gamow. Great physicist's fascinating, readable overview of contemporary science: number theory, relativity, fourth dimension, entropy, genes, atomic structure, much more. 128 illustrations. Index. 352pp. 5⅜ x 8½.   25664-2 Pa. $8.95

ENGINEERING IN HISTORY, Richard Shelton Kirby, et al. Broad, nontechnical survey of history's major technological advances: birth of Greek science, industrial revolution, electricity and applied science, 20th-century automation, much more. 181 illustrations. ". . . excellent . . ."–*Isis.* Bibliography. vii + 530pp. 5⅜ x 8¼.   26412-2 Pa. $14.95

DALÍ ON MODERN ART: The Cuckolds of Antiquated Modern Art, Salvador Dalí. Influential painter skewers modern art and its practitioners. Outrageous evaluations of Picasso, Cézanne, Turner, more. 15 renderings of paintings discussed. 44 calligraphic decorations by Dalí. 96pp. 5⅜ x 8½. (USO)   29220-7 Pa. $4.95

ANTIQUE PLAYING CARDS: A Pictorial History, Henry René D'Allemagne. Over 900 elaborate, decorative images from rare playing cards (14th–20th centuries): Bacchus, death, dancing dogs, hunting scenes, royal coats of arms, players cheating, much more. 96pp. 9¼ x 12¼.   29265-7 Pa. $11.95

MAKING FURNITURE MASTERPIECES: 30 Projects with Measured Drawings, Franklin H. Gottshall. Step-by-step instructions, illustrations for constructing handsome, useful pieces, among them a Sheraton desk, Chippendale chair, Spanish desk, Queen Anne table and a William and Mary dressing mirror. 224pp. 8⅛ x 11¼.   29338-6 Pa. $13.95

THE FOSSIL BOOK: A Record of Prehistoric Life, Patricia V. Rich et al. Profusely illustrated definitive guide covers everything from single-celled organisms and dinosaurs to birds and mammals and the interplay between climate and man. Over 1,500 illustrations. 760pp. 7½ x 10⅛.   29371-8 Pa. $29.95

Prices subject to change without notice.

Available at your book dealer or write for free catalog to Dept. GI, Dover Publications, Inc., 31 East 2nd St., Mineola, N.Y. 11501. Dover publishes more than 500 books each year on science, elementary and advanced mathematics, biology, music, art, literary history, social sciences and other areas.